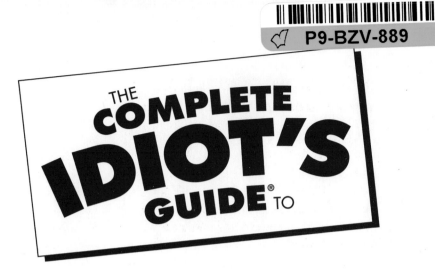

THE
COMPLETE
IDIOT'S
GUIDE® TO

Zombies

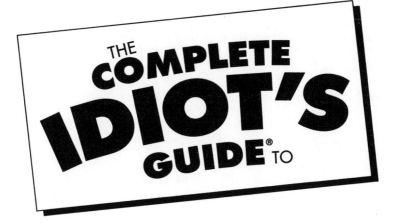

Zombies

by Nathan Robert Brown

ALPHA

A member of Penguin Group (USA) Inc.

This book is dedicated to my wonderful agent, Jacky Sach, to whom I will always be grateful for giving a young writer a chance almost 10 years ago. All my best to you in your future endeavors. You will be sincerely missed. This book is also dedicated to the legend himself, George A. Romero.

ALPHA BOOKS

Published by the Penguin Group

Penguin Group (USA) Inc., 375 Hudson Street, New York, New York 10014, USA

Penguin Group (Canada), 10 Alcorn Avenue, Toronto, Ontario, Canada M4V 3B2 (a division of Pearson Penguin Canada Inc.)

Penguin Books Ltd., 80 Strand, London WC2R 0RL, England

Penguin Ireland, 25 St. Stephen's Green, Dublin 2, Ireland (a division of Penguin Books Ltd.)

Penguin Group (Australia), 250 Camberwell Road, Camberwell, Victoria 3124, Australia (a division of Pearson Australia Group Pty. Ltd.)

Penguin Books India Pvt. Ltd., 11 Community Centre, Panchsheel Park, New Delhi—10 017, India

Penguin Group (NZ), cnr. Airborne and Rosedale roads, Albany, Auckland 1310, New Zealand (a division of Pearson New Zealand Ltd.)

Penguin Books (South Africa) (Pty.) Ltd., 24 Sturdee Avenue, Rosebank, Johannesburg 2196, South Africa

Penguin Books Ltd., Registered Offices: 80 Strand, London WC2R 0RL, England

International Standard Book Number: 978-1-61564-014-0
Library of Congress Catalog Card Number: 2009937016

12   11   10   8   7   6   5   4   3   2   1

Interpretation of the printing code: The rightmost number of the first series of numbers is the year of the book's printing; the rightmost number of the second series of numbers is the number of the book's printing. For example, a printing code of 10-1 shows that the first printing occurred in 2010.

Printed in the United States of America

Note: This publication contains the opinions and ideas of its author. It is intended to provide helpful and informative material on the subject matter covered. It is sold with the understanding that the author and publisher are not engaged in rendering professional services in the book. If the reader requires personal assistance or advice, a competent professional should be consulted.

The author and publisher specifically disclaim any responsibility for any liability, loss, or risk, personal or otherwise, which is incurred as a consequence, directly or indirectly, of the use and application of any of the contents of this book.

Most Alpha books are available at special quantity discounts for bulk purchases for sales promotions, premiums, fund-raising, or educational use. Special books, or book excerpts, can also be created to fit specific needs.

For details, write: Special Markets, Alpha Books, 375 Hudson Street, New York, NY 10014.

Publisher: *Marie Butler-Knight*
Editorial Director: *Mike Sanders*
Senior Managing Editor: *Billy Fields*
Executive Editor: *Randy Ladenheim-Gil*
Development Editor: *Megan Douglass*
Production Editor: *Kayla Dugger*

Copy Editor: *Krista Hansing Editorial Services, Inc.*
Cover Designer: *Bill Thomas*
Book Designer: *Trina Wurst*
Indexer: *Johnna VanHoose Dinse*
Layout: *Ayanna Lacey*
Proofreader: *Laura Caddell*

Contents at a Glance

   *Never in the history of literature have zombies
   had such an overwhelming presence as they now
   enjoy. The last two decades could certainly be
   labeled by later generations as the Zombie Age
   of literature, and since 1990 the undead have
   begun to cross the genre boundary of horror fiction into other areas.*

   *From the United States to Europe to Japan,
   the undead have overrun the illustrated world
   of Western comic books, Japanese manga, and
   international graphic novels. There are now
   alternate zombie universes, zombie virus–
   infected superheroes, and even stories depicting
   intelligent zombies invading this world from an
   alternate dimension.*

   *In recent years, a number of popular titles have
   emerged that have zombies at their cores. From
   serious to comical, to a little bit of both, zombie-
   themed web comics have taken the net by storm.
   A simple web search will yield enough results
   to fill up a book. This chapter offers but a sampling of the zombie web comic titles available.*

   *Zombies first entered the world of moving pic-
   tures in the twentieth century and have only
   grown in popularity since. Many of these early
   zombie films were set in the Caribbean Islands
   to give them a more "authentic" feel. Some
   of these early zombie movies even brought the
   walking dead into the realm of comedy for the
   very first time.*

Appendixes

Contents

Appendixes

Introduction

Death has often been called "the great equalizer." It comes for us all, and none of us are exempt from its cold and final embrace. The reality of death is it's one of the very few undeniable and absolute truths of human existence. Perhaps this is why the idea of something that could trump this great truth is so terrifying and intriguing to us. What could humanity do if death ceased to be the final destination of the living?

For the last half-century, the living dead have thrived in our imaginations as the embodiment of all that we as human beings fear and despise. They come for us with gnashing teeth, and their bite is a curse of walking death. But these harbingers of Armageddon are seen as neither angels of death nor grim reapers. No, the undead hordes are shown as made up of our neighbors, our families, and our friends. And no matter how much we loved them during life, they have but one motivating desire … to devour us and, in so doing, share with us their curse of undeath.

Not since arriving in the late 1960s have modern zombies had such a strong presence in pop culture. The living dead, figuratively speaking, are everywhere. And perhaps this should not be surprising. At a time when the world is in chaos, zombies have always arisen in the collective imagination of human beings.

In the late '60s, the world seemed to be falling ever deeper into despair and chaos. The United States was involved in an increasingly unsustainable "conflict" in Vietnam, fighting an enemy the likes of which had never been engaged. And the rising cost of this war was being worsened by soaring inflation rates, leading to a surge of civil unrest back home. And the Vietnam conflict was not the only issue on which the country was divided in opinion.

Martin Luther King Jr. led a movement for civil rights, bringing an end to the racial segregation that still occurred throughout the country. In their homes, Americans watched National Guardsmen spray trapped children with fire hoses. They watched as the "Days of Rage" race riots ripped the city of York, Pennsylvania, to shreds. And they watched as King's peaceful quest for racial equality ended in his assassination. However, he was not the only great man of the time to die at the hands of assassins. The American people also witnessed, live on their television sets, the assassinations of President John F. Kennedy and, shortly after, his younger brother Robert Kennedy. By 1968, it seemed as if the world had gone mad.

So why have the zombies returned to the American imagination with such fervor? And why now? Perhaps the answer to this lies in what has already been discussed. After all, the world of today is much like the world of 1968. The world is suffering from issues of sustainability, experiencing crises of finance and energy. The United States is involved in an increasingly unsustainable, two-front war against an enemy who fights with unprecedented guerilla/terrorist tactics. And on all these issues, the American people seem almost evenly divided in their opinions. Once again, it seems as if the entire world is losing its mind.

But why would zombies be so prevalent in the imaginations of the people at times of general chaos and uncertainty? Simply put, the living dead represent the absolute worst-case scenario for humankind. Nothing else even comes close to matching the desperate odds humanity would face in a zombie apocalypse. Zombies are the one thing that makes our world, no matter how insane it has become, seem ... well ... not so bad. Think of it this way. No matter how bad the world gets, zombies will always be there to offer us a twisted bright side. After all, things could be much worse ... the world could be overrun by hordes of homicidal living dead.

How to Use This Book

To offer a more effective and user-friendly reference on the many fascinating and gory facets of the living dead, I've separated this book into four main parts. These parts are then further broken down into chapters by their respective subjects and types. The basic organization of *The Complete Idiot's Guide to Zombies* can be summed up as follows:

In **Part 1, "The Zombie Shift,"** we begin by taking a look at the history of the living dead. From the dark rituals of Haitian Voodoo and ancient superstitions to the rise of radiation fears and virus phobias, zombies have always represented the worst elements of human civilization. In this part, we examine this relationship between the living and the dead—between them and us. After all, in the end, it just might turn out that they *are* us.

In **Part 2, "Zombie Literature and Comics,"** we look at how zombies have been depicted in both written and illustrated forms. For the last hundred years, the idea of reanimating the dead has captivated the imaginations of countless readers of literature and comics alike. In the more modern medium of web comics, zombies have continued to exhibit a strong presence.

Part 3, "Zombie Cinema and Pop Culture," examines the modern treatments of zombies in various aspects of modern culture. This part starts with a chapter discussing the first zombie films ever made. This will be followed up with a look into the works of George A. Romero, who sparked the modern zombie phenomenon in 1968 with his classic film *Night of the Living Dead*. It also looks at the many non-Romero zombie films (the good, the bad, and the ugly), as well as zombie-themed video games past and present.

Part 4, "Zombies and Us," takes a look at the world of zombie fandom and the subculture of zombie survivalist groups. Zombies have a very real place in our modern world. For some, they offer a fun medium for social commentary. For others, the living dead offer a worst-case survival scenario, the preparation for which makes you ready to tackle the worst that reality could throw at you.

Extras

Moooooaaaaan...

These sidebars offer definitions and explanations for the various terms you will encounter in your reading.

Don't Get Bit!

These sidebars offer clarification for easily confused concepts, events, and words related to zombies, such as common misperceptions and similarities in spellings, plots, purposes, or actions.

Brains!

These sidebars offer facts related to the content of the text. Some of these simply offer interesting but extraneous side notes; others are directly related to the subject matter.

Anyone Smell That?

Sometimes the line between reality and fiction can become a little blurred. These sidebars act as reality checks, offering rational explanations for seemingly spectacular situations.

Acknowledgments

As always, I would like to thank everyone at Alpha Books who made this project possible. A special thanks to Randy Ladenheim-Gil and Megan Douglass for their amazing patience and unbending confidence. I would also like to thank Dr. Margaret Lowry and Dr. Tim Morris, as well as the entire English Department at University of Texas at Arlington, for putting up with my sporadic stress fits and general state of anxiety during this book's completion.

Trademarks

All terms mentioned in this book that are known to be or are suspected of being trademarks or service marks have been appropriately capitalized. Alpha Books and Penguin Group (USA) Inc. cannot attest to the accuracy of this information. Use of a term in this book should not be regarded as affecting the validity of any trademark or service mark.

Part 1

The Zombie Shift

Where did the concept of zombies, those reanimated corpses that frighten us, come from? Many would point to the strange practices of Voodoo to answer this question. While this is certainly where we acquired the word *zombie*, it fails to answer the entirety of the question—how did they come to be the flesh-eating, murderous walking dead? In Part 1, we examine the "evolution of undeath." From superstition, to radiation, to viral mutation, zombies are always the result of that which is most real and frightening in the collective human psyche. And as we all know, the face of fear changes with the times.

Chapter 1

The Voodoo Zombie

In This Chapter

- The West African origins of the initial zombie concept
- The Zombification practice of Haitian Vodun
- The active ingredients in Vodun's so-called "zombie powder"
- Known victims of the Haitian zombie powder
- The specific behaviors of Vodun zombies
- The horrific facts regarding Voodoo Zombification

Even the walking dead had to begin somewhere. Many of the fearsome figures that horrify the human mind can be traced to some mythic or superstitious origin, and the zombie is no exception. While the modern pop culture concept of the zombie bears little resemblance to its progenitor, the relationship between them is certainly worthy of discussion. This chapter explains where the term *zombie* came from and explores the profound effect it has had on many preconceived beliefs about life and death.

Zombie Origins

Where did we get the word *zombie*? Well, we got it from the Haitian Voodoo (proper spelling is *Vodun*) term *zombi*. They, in turn, got it from a West African term of the Yoruba tribe. In its original Yoruba usage, *zombi* could potentially be used to refer to two things—the name of a snake/python god or particular leading members of the snake/python god cult. The name of the *Zombi* snake god made its way to the island of Haiti (as well as other Caribbean islands), on the tongues of Yoruba tribesman whom French colonists had enslaved to work on their sugar cane plantations. As the years passed, the indigenous spiritual traditions of these slaves became integrated with various symbols and concepts from Christianity/Catholicism. Eventually, this practice came to be known as what is now called Vodun (commonly referred to by most non-Haitians as "Voodoo"). The meaning of the word *zombi*, however, had changed by the time it became part of the vocabulary of the pigeon French-African language of Haiti, known as Creole.

Mooooooaaaaan...

Vodun is the root term of the Western word *Voodoo*. The term comes from Africa and literally means "spirit." In the proper context, however, it refers to certain indigenous African religious ritual practices that were meant for communicating with or invoking the power of ancestral spirits, divine forces, or malevolent entities. The purpose of such practices was either beneficial (such as for healing or fertility) or destructive (curses, war, and so on).

In the Creole vocabulary, the name of the snake god was changed to *Damballah*, thus replacing the name *Zombi*. The significant role of Damballah in the Haitian Vodun creation myth, "The Serpent and the Rainbow," is discussed in detail later on in this chapter. The spirit of the Damballah snake deity is also invoked during the process of creating zombie powder and, therefore, is considered directly related to the creation of a Vodun *zombi*. So it stands to reason that the old name of the god came to refer to those who were said to have suffered his wrath.

In Haitian Vodun, a *zombi* is believed to be one whose soul has been imprisoned, stolen, or destroyed by a Vodun priest or priestess, causing them to enter a state of "temporary death." According to Vodun belief, the acting priest or priestess could then reanimate and control the person's body like a slave. After his or her reanimation, a Vodun *zombi* was said to be bound in the service of the one who killed and resurrected him or her.

In the twentieth century, Haitian governmental authorities wanted to end the Vodun *zombi* practice, as well as diminish the power that Vodun practitioners exerted over their communities. One notable act the authorities took was to outlaw the creation of a Vodun *zombi*. Even today, the Haitian penal code expressly outlaws what it terms as the practice of "Zombie-ism."

As in most magical practices, Vodun includes the idea of cosmic balance (a concept similar to that of Karma in Buddhism and Hinduism). Basically, this belief states that what one creates will influence what one receives. This means that performing rituals or spells for healings and other beneficial purposes will result in a return of good things. In contrast, performing malevolent or destructive spells or rituals will ultimately result in a return of bad things. Because of this, nearly all *houngan* and *mambo* restrict themselves largely to only beneficial rituals and spells, carried out in their respective *humforts*. Those who do not are called *bokors* or *caplatas* and are said to practice their arts on the "left hand" of Vodun (referring to the nonbeneficial nature of their magic).

Mooooaaaaan...

Vodun priests are called by the title of **houngan,** and priestesses are referred to as **mambo.**

Each Vodun practitioner keeps a temple or shrine, called a **humfort,** which can be as large as a building or as small as a shelf top. The *humfort* is commonly located in their homes or in a small apartment where they meet with "clients," or those seeking their services.

The Zombie Journey of Wade Davis

Probably the most well-known modern chronicler of the Voodoo *zombi* phenomenon is a Canadian ethnobotanist and researcher named Wade Davis. After hearing reports of Haitian Vodun priests resurrecting the dead and enslaving them, Davis personally traveled to Haiti to discover the truth. He hypothesized that perhaps some narcotic or unknown compound allowed the priests to make a person appear to be dead and that they then used some form of hallucinogen to control their victims. He chronicled his journey into the elusive world of Haitian Vodun in a book he entitled *The Serpent and the Rainbow*, which in 1988 was adapted by horror director Wes Craven into a rather sensationalized film version (unfortunately, most people are more familiar with the film than with Davis's written works).

Initially, Davis went to Haiti with the (somewhat incorrect) theory that this so-called "zombie powder" contained a powerful hallucinogen called Calabar (or Calabar bean) that was used in violently severe spiritual rituals among certain tribes of West Africa. He also theorized that a similar plant, called datura, might also be involved (or used in conjunction with Calabar). He learned that Haitian locals even referred to the datura plant as the "*zombi* cucumber." Both substances are said to produce horrific, nightmarish visions that throw one into a state of temporary and violent madness (which, according to the spiritual tradition, resulted from the user coming into direct contact with the world of the gods and ruling spirits). However, after an initial search of the island, Davis discovered that very little of the naturally growing species of Calabar and datura were readily available on the island, and certainly not in sufficient enough quantities to induce the altered state that Davis referred to as "Zombification."

Eventually, and after many fruitless attempts (he was "duped" several times, discovering later that he'd been sold fake or inactive versions of the zombie powder substance), Davis managed to get his hands on a sample of genuine zombie powder. He identified the presence of a highly potent and potentially fatal neurotoxin that was extracted from the organs of a small local species of puffer fish. This substance, called tetrodotoxin (abbreviated as TTX), is highly toxic and hard to handle safely. Even briefly touching TTX is dangerous, since it can be absorbed easily through the skin. TTX can induce a state of such extreme paralysis that one's vital signs are reduced to nearly undetectable levels.

** By the Way**

Today many of the people who are accidentally exposed to TTX are not victims of Zombification. In fact, most exposures are caused by improper preparation of Japanese puffer fish, which is considered a delicacy. It is also very expensive, since one needs a special culinary license just to prepare and serve it. Because of this, there is a market for unlicensed "black market" puffer fish meat. Often ingesting this is a deadly game of chance ... and one that is certainly not recommended.

Nine times out of ten, human exposure to TTX is fatal. If you don't believe it, just do a simple web search and you will find countless horror stories of people who accidentally came into contact with the substance and nearly died. However, if a small-enough dose is administered, the person essentially appears dead. Many recorded victims of Zombification have even been mistakenly pronounced dead by those who would qualify as trained medical professionals. Without special instruments, there is no way to know that the person is still alive.

The Serpent and the Rainbow

While many people are certainly familiar with at least the title of Wade Davis's novel (or, at least, the movie adaptation) *The Serpent and the Rainbow*, few truly know what it refers to. "The Serpent and the Rainbow" is a reference to a *primal myth* of the Vodun religion, which (like many such myths) tells of a divine marriage between a cosmic serpent, Damballah, and the rainbow, Ayida Wedo. Their union, according to the myth, resulted in the creation of the world as we know it.

Mooooaaaaan...

A **primal myth** is a myth upon which all others in a tradition are based. It usually deals with how the world or humanity was created. These myths commonly incorporate the symbols of trees, serpents, and male-female unions.

The myth of "The Serpent and the Rainbow" can commonly be summed up as follows:

The Ancients (probably a reference to the unknown first tellers of the myth) said that, in the beginning, there was only the Great Serpent

Damballah. With his 7,000 coils, Damballah supported Earth so that it would not be lost in the great abyss (referred to in some translations as the "endless sea"). The time came for Damballah to shed his skin, so he began to move in order to slough off a layer of it. This shed layer spiraled upward until it had wrapped around what we call the "Universe." From its falling scales came forth the stars and all that which dwells in the heavens. As they hit Earth, the scales sparked the violent process of Creation. Unimaginable storms whipped up, and Earth was covered by volcanic eruptions, from which were formed the metals and other such elements. The heat rose into the sky and caused great bolts of lightning to strike the surface of Earth, which resulted in the creation of certain sacred stones. When things began to quiet, Damballah wished to look upon this new creation. He stretched himself out upon the path of the sun and, for a time, drank of its essence.

With the many layers of Damballah's skin was the Spring of Immortality (or Eternal Life), which he then poured forth across the surface of the newly formed Earth so that life might begin. As the water struck against the dry surface of Earth, its spray was struck by the light of the sun and Ayida Wedo (Rainbow) was born. Seeing her beauty, Damballah took her as his wife. He wrapped around her and their love was consummated. From their union came the life-giving, divine substance (more specifically, the substance from which the myth says blood, milk, and semen came). They showed the innocent humans below, who had been born of the blood, how to use these substances to their benefit. Women learned to produce the divine substance (milk) in their breasts, to nurse their young. Men learned to create and store the divine substance (semen) in their testicles. Then Damballah and Ayida Wedo taught the men how to "damn the flow of the women's blood" (a reference to menstruation) to create new life. Before returning to the heavens, Damballah and Ayida Wedo taught the humans to partake of the blood as a holy sacrament so that they might not forget the Divine Wisdom of the Serpent and the Rainbow.

The Zombification Files

In recent years, increasing attention has been given to past reports of Zombification, especially those coming out of Haiti. Before the recent discoveries regarding the role of neurotoxins and hallucinogenic sub-stances in the so-called "zombie powders," such stories had long been dismissed as nothing more than baseless stories fueled by superstitious beliefs.

The number of stories about people whom Vodun devotees made zom-bies is numerous in the mythos of Haitian culture. However, it is often difficult to separate the true stories from the fictional ones. What fol-lows are five specific Zombification cases from different parts of Haiti, each of which were recorded by individuals who are considered fairly credible. Please remember, these cases are not thought to be accounts of the true "walking dead," but are cases of individuals who are believed to have been exposed to a highly dangerous cocktail of potent neuro-toxins (namely, puffer fish poison) and hallucinogenic substances (likely Calabar beans or datura, or some combination of the two).

Case 1—The Reluctant Father (1898)

The following account was recorded by Zora Neale Hurston in her work *Tell My Horse*, published in 1981 … though previously it had been printed (somewhat briefly) in 1937 but had not been well received due to the widespread prejudicial attitudes of the time toward black and female authors (Hurston was both). This story illustrates a rather common element in the Haitian understanding of the Vodun *zombi*, which is often seen as a righteous punishment for people who do not do what the community expects of them (although there are certainly many *zombi* cases in which this was not the case), such as not keeping one's contractual obligations or refusing to take responsibility for one's actions (especially if those actions affect others in the community).

According to Hurston's account of the story, this case of Zombification took place during the last years of the nineteenth century (she claims 1898) in the Haitian region of Cap Haitien. This case involves a young local who, after having gotten a female acquaintance pregnant, refused to take any responsibility for the mother and child. The girl's family, hoping to come to some agreement, held a meeting with the boy's fam-ily. Despite their appeals, the family offered nothing to the pregnant girl (they probably believed their son, who claimed the child couldn't be his). A couple weeks after the fruitless meeting between the families, the young man in question fell ill and suddenly died (which is usually what happens in cases of Zombification). As was the custom, a funeral was immediately held and the young man was buried.

Months passed, and no one suspected that the boy had been a victim of Zombification until, one day, his mother passed a group of day laborers during a trip to the city. The face of one laborer caught her attention as he unloaded a heavy bag of coffee beans onto a truck. She immediately recognized the man as her son! He looked her right in the eyes, but his face showed no signs of recognition. He only stared blankly before continuing his work. The mother ran to get help. By the time she returned, however, the man she claimed was her son was nowhere to be seen. When questioned, the foreman denied ever having employed a laborer matching the woman's description. The mother never saw her son again.

In this case, the family of the pregnant girl likely took their appeal to a Vodun priest (*houngan*) or priestess (*mambo*). The Vodun probably offered to make a zombie of the boy, who could then be rented out (or even sold) as a day laborer to provide some form of restitution for the costs of the birth and child-rearing. However, no such case was ever tried … likely because no evidence existed to prove that a man who was supposedly dead was actually working in the city. In all honesty, the young-man-turned-*zombi* (if indeed the man the mother saw had been him) was likely either killed or sold to foreign traders soon after his mother recognized him.

Case 2—The *Zombi* Bride (Exact Date Unknown)

This account was first recorded by Alfred Metraux, in his 1972 work *Voodoo in Haiti* (a text that most experts consider to be a fair and objective treatment of the subject). This report involves a young girl who, even though she was already betrothed, became the object of a *houngan* priest's desires. When she spurned his advances, the priest muttered a threat of revenge and vowed that he would possess her, one way or another. Days later, the young woman fell mysteriously ill and suddenly died.

On the day of her burial, it was realized that the measurements of the coffin were not quite adequate to accommodate her height. To make the body fit into the available space, the girl's neck had to be bent sharply to one side. During the preburial viewing of her body, a relative accidentally dropped a lit cigarette into the coffin, causing a small but serious burn on the top of one of her feet.

Months later, rumors reached the girl's village that she had been seen in a nearby city. To make things worse, she was said to have been in the company of the *houngan* priest who had vowed that he would have her. Few of the villagers believed these rumors at first. They quickly changed their minds when, a few months later, the girl, very much alive, wandered into her home village. She was in a state of dementia and was so emaciated that she might not have been recognizable had it not been for two identifying marks. Due to the way her head had been shoved into the coffin, the girl's neck was somewhat deformed. And on the top of one foot was the scar from the careless cigarette burn she'd received during her wake.

It turned out that the *houngan* priest, realizing he'd been seen with the girl and fearing criminal prosecution, had decided to free all of his zombies (apparently, he had created multiple *zombi* servants over the years). At this particular time, Haitian judicial authorities had declared it a serious crime to create a *zombi* and were cracking down on such practices as part of what could be called a "de-superstition" or "anti-superstition" campaign. Though the girl gained her freedom and was reunited with her family, this story does not exactly have a happy ending. Her brain damage and the resulting dementia turned out to be permanent. She never recovered from her Zombification.

Case 3—The Zombification of Marie M. (1909)

This is another case that was recorded in Zora Neale Hurston's *Tell My Horse*. It became one of the more well-known cases of Zombification reported during the early twentieth century. The popularity of the report was likely due to the fact that the alleged victim, identified as Marie M., was said to have been the daughter of one of Haiti's most affluent families (the name of the family, however, is never specified) in the capital city of Port-au-Prince.

Anyone Smell That?

Often victims of Vodun Zombification are said to move clumsily, speak with slurred speech, and exhibit inattentive or "spacey" behavior. Researchers now believe that these symptoms are the likely result of permanent brain damage, caused by a combination of prolonged oxygen deprivation (during the time they are buried alive) and exposure to the neurotoxin TTX and the hallucinogenic effects of datura or Calabar.

It is generally agreed that Marie M. was pronounced dead and buried sometime in October 1909. For years, nothing seemed out of the ordinary about the situation. About five years after her burial, however, a group of frantic girls (former classmates of Marie) reported that they had seen Marie looking out of the window of what was thought to be an abandoned house. Others had also reported seeing a girl in the house. Neighbors and relatives implored the father to get the police to serve a search warrant on the property. He hesitated for several days before finally giving in and requesting the warrant. By the time the police arrived, the girl was nowhere to be found. Many in the community suspected that the father knew more than he was telling.

Facing public scrutiny, the local Port-au-Prince justice authorities ordered that the girl's body be exhumed and examined to confirm her death. When the coffin was dug up and opened, however, the girl's burial clothes were found neatly folded beside a set of skeletal remains that were obviously not Marie's. The skeleton was far too big for the coffin (designed for a young girl) and so was twisted in an unnatural position. Once again, authorities turned to the father for answers.

The Port-au-Prince newspapers later reported that the father had explained that he'd learned his daughter had been the victim of a local *houngan* priest. The priest had recently died, and his widow turned the girl over to the local church. The church then informed the girl's father what had happened (which, as one can imagine, came as quite a shock). Since their family was powerful and frequently in the public eye, Marie's father (wishing to avoid a public scandal) had kept her hidden in the old house until he could arrange for her passage to a foreign country, where he planned to have her treated by expert physicians. Most of the reports claimed that Marie M. quickly recovered under this treatment and afterward lived out the rest of her life overseas.

Anyone Smell That?

Vodun practices are based on belief and superstition. So even *houngans* and *mambos* must adhere to the laws they claim rule their world. This is why a *houngan's* widow would release his *zombi* slaves. It was believed that a *zombi* was a person whose soul had been imprisoned, banished, or destroyed by a *houngan* or *mambo*. However, superstition states that the soul is returned to the victim upon the creator's death. Therefore, using any *zombi* as a servant after the *houngan's* or *mambo's* death would risk retribution from others for violating Vodun laws.

Case 4—*Ti Femme* (1979)

This particular Zombification case was first chronicled by Wade Davis in his 1985 work *The Serpent and the Rainbow* and was examined in further detail in his 1998 book *Passage of Darkness*. The victim in this case was a Haitian woman by the name of Francina Illeus. However, she is known throughout the modern *zombi* legends of Haiti as *Ti Femme*, or "The Woman."

After suffering for weeks with an unidentified digestive illness, Francina's family took her to the nearby Michel de l'Atalaye Hospital. After a few days, she seemed to improve and was discharged. Within days, however, her condition took a sudden turn for the worse and she died at her home. A local magistrate examined her body; pronounced Francina dead on February 23, 1976; and wrote up a death certificate. She was only 30 years old.

Just over three years later, in April 1979, a strange, empty-eyed woman was sighted wandering aimlessly through the market district of Ennery. The locals were well aware that the woman was a *zombi* and steered cleared of her. They did, however, report the woman to an American missionary by the name of Jay Ausherman. Following their reports, Ausherman eventually found the woman who would later turn out to be the allegedly dead Francina Illeus. She was huddled in a corner, skinny as a rail, clothed in tatters, with her bony hands crossed in front of her face. Some locals recognized Francina and explained to Ausherman that she had been buried some three years earlier.

Francina was taken to the presiding judge of Ennery, who had no idea what to do with her (after all, she was supposed to be dead and, according to official records, she still was). The judge was therefore more than willing to simply hand her over to Ausherman, who took her to see psychiatrist and physician Dr. Lamarque Douyon at the *Centre de Psychiatrie et Neurologie Mars-Kline* (Mars-Kline Psychiatric and Neurological Center) in the capital city of Port-au-Prince. In his evaluation, Dr. Douyon found that Francina was suffering from malnutrition and had been stricken mute. Dr. Douyon was no stranger to the terrible effects of Zombification, of course, as he'd dealt with such patients before and knew that these people were certainly not the walking dead. Unfortunately, this was neither the first nor the last time that he would treat a victim of Vodun Zombification.

Despite the risk of retribution from members of the Vodun cult, Dr. Douyon worked tirelessly to uncover the truth behind what had happened to the poor woman. He learned from relatives that it was generally believed that Francina's husband had contracted the services of a *houngan* during a fit of jealousy (a behavior he appeared rather prone to exhibit) to have his wife made into a *zombi*. To verify that he was not just the victim of some elaborate hoax or sick prank, the courts granted Dr. Douyon permission to have Francina's coffin exhumed. When it was opened, no body was found inside. The *houngan* had not even tried to use a substitute corpse ... nothing more than a pile of heavy stones was inside.

Case 5—Clairvius Narcisse (1980)

The case of Clairvius Narcisse, also recorded by Wade Davis, was not discovered until 1980. The poor man's Zombification ordeal, however, had actually begun way back in 1962. Clairvius was 40 years old in 1962 when, on the night of April 30, he suddenly became violently ill and had to be rushed to the Albert Schweitzer Hospital in the central Haitian city of Deschapelles. His fever was terribly high and his entire body hurt. Within hours, he was vomiting blood.

In a matter of days, the hospital doctors (one of whom was a well-educated American physician) pronounced Clairvius dead. His sister Angelica witnessed the scene. Clairvius's body was officially identified by his elder sister, Marie Claire, and a death certificate was promptly written up. Clairvius's body was placed in cold storage for nearly an entire day (20 hours) before his body was released for burial, which was carried out immediately. It took 10 days for a large, stone memorial slab to be completed and placed over his gravesite by certain members of his family. For the next 18 years, Clairvius was counted among the dead by those who had known him in life.

In 1980, Angelica Narcisse, the man's sister, was shopping in the marketplace in L'Estere, Haiti, when she was approached by a man who introduced himself with the private nickname that she'd once called Clairvius. He explained to her that he was, in fact, the brother that she'd long believed to be dead. He then conveyed to her the horrifying details of what had become of him since.

Brains!

The story of Clairvius Narcisse's experience of Zombification has received more media attention than any other such case in modern history. Within a year of his "return to life," the BBC sent a film crew to Haiti to shoot a short documentary about him.

Clairvius told Angelica that he'd learned his brother had contracted the service of a *houngan* who used dark magic, called a "bokor." The brother had done this because he had refused to sell his part of a land inheritance (which, by law, was distributed equally among male siblings). Clairvius had later awakened in his coffin to the chants of the bokor who had poisoned him (although Clairvius truly believed his soul had been taken), a victim of Zombification. He had been beaten severely and tied up by both the bokor and his attendants before being led away to work in a place in northern Haiti as a slave (and, he explained, in a team alongside many of the bokor's other *zombi* victims). After only two years as a *zombi* slave, the bokor holding Clairvius and the others either had died or been killed, thereby freeing them all from his control. However, Clairvius had not dared return home because he knew that the same brother who had given him to the bokor was still alive and would likely have him killed. So for 16 years, Clairvius had wandered Haiti as a beggar, until one day he had learned that his spiteful brother had finally died. Feeling that it was now safe, Clairvius had sought out his sister Angelica.

As have many survivors of Zombification, Clairvius sought out Dr. Lamarque Douyon for treatment and assistance. Douyon did his best to find ways to verify the man's story, but after so many years, he could do little. Like many poor Haitians, Clairvius had never even been to a dentist, so identifying him that way was impossible. Checking his coffin would not prove anything, since it was common practice for *houngan* priests to leave behind a substitute corpse. In addition, DNA analysis was still a *very* young science in 1980 and certainly was not yet available to Haitian laboratories. It appeared, however, that the man had little to gain by pretending to be someone he was not. The Narcisse family was extremely poor, so he certainly didn't expect to gain money.

In the end, the best method of identification Dr. Douyon could think of was to first interview Clairvius's closest relatives. Based on these interviews, he produced a list of questions that not even his relatives could answer in entirety. The man claiming to be Clairvius correctly answered every single one of the questions about his past. While Clairvius was able to live out the rest of his days in relative happiness with his loved ones—and regained his sanity—he suffered mild but permanent brain damage as a result of his Zombification. One final sad element to this story is that Clairvius truly believed that the *houngan* had temporarily stolen his soul and that, for a time, he had been a walking dead man. The fact that Clairvius did not realize that he had not actually been brought back from the dead has, oddly enough, caused many people to criticize Davis's theories about his condition altogether.

A Horrific Truth

The horrific thought of zombie powder is even worse if you consider what it would be like to experience it firsthand. Imagine what it must be like to be a victim of this substance. First, the powder is slipped to you (likely in such a way that you are not even aware of it), probably through skin contact (it has been said that the skin of the left forearm is the ideal target due to its proximity to the heart).

Shortly after being exposed, you become violently ill. You find it hard to breathe. Before you realize what is happening, your entire body is completely gripped by paralysis. You can't move. You can't speak. You can't do anything. Everyone around you believes you are stone dead. To make matters worse, you can still see, hear, and feel *everything* that is happening.

The doctor comes in and checks your vital signs, probably just by checking your pulse with his fingers. Unfortunately for you, your pulse is so slow and faint that the doctor doesn't even feel it. You lay there helpless as he declares your time of death for your death certificate. Your mind is screaming out to them, "I'm not dead!" Your body, however, is no longer able to listen to your commands.

As you are moved onto a slab and rolled out of the room, you are completely aware. You know full well what's going on as they take you to the ambulance, coroner's van, funeral home, or morgue. If you are lucky, you live in one of the few parts of the world (such as Haiti) where they frequently bury the dead without performing autopsies or embalming the bodies. If you are not, however, this means you will be fully able to experience the pain and horror of having an autopsy or embalming procedure performed on you … while you are still alive and still feeling everything. You'll feel it when the coroner slices you open, cracks open your ribcage, and begins removing your internal organs. Even if an autopsy is not performed, you'll feel it when the funeral director replaces your blood with formaldehyde. And the entire time, you won't be able to do anything but lie there motionless in your silent agony.

If you are a victim of a Haitian Vodun Zombification and have not been killed by autopsy or embalmment, you will soon be buried alive. As the oxygen levels in your coffin reach dangerously low levels, you lose consciousness. Soon, however, you awaken to the chants of the *houngan* or *mambo* who did this to you. The poison has begun to wear off, but the hallucinogens are in full effect. You are also likely weak and mildly brain-damaged at this point, and the *houngan* or *mambo* tells you that you have been raised from the dead and must now serve him or her until the day he or she dies. Because of your diminished mental faculties, not to mention the influence of hallucinogens, you likely believe this.

In recent years, researchers of the Vodun zombie powder have made a frightening discovery. Most claim that it is miraculous anyone could survive this process of Zombification.

Research into the effects of what most now believe are the actual contents of zombie powder has also revealed some interesting data regarding its success rate. In truth, anyone employing this substance would likely succeed in making only about 1 zombie for every 100 or more attempts. The other 99-plus times, they would only succeed in killing their victims. This means that for every confirmed victim of Vodun Zombification, the acting *houngan* or *mambo* has killed roughly 99 additional people. So many deaths, all because some power-hungry, poison-using con artist posing as a spiritual magic-user wanted to have a subservient, brain-damaged slave.

The Least You Need to Know

- The zombie root word *zombi* is believed to have originated in West Africa as the name of a snake god or snake god cult.

- Vodun/Voodoo zombies are not the living dead, but people who have been made to appear dead.

- Zombie powder is likely some combination of the active ingredients TTX, datura, and Calabar.

- Only over the last century has the truth about Voodoo Zombification been realized.

- Current research shows that only about 1 in every 100 attempts at Zombification would likely be successful.

2

The Rise of the Living Dead

In This Chapter

- ◆ The transition of zombie lore in the twentieth century
- ◆ The Atomic Age reign of the groundbreaking "radiation zombie"
- ◆ The widespread depiction of the "viral zombie" in recent years
- ◆ The role of the human brain in zombie lore
- ◆ The primary types of modern zombies found in pop culture

How did the zombie as we know it come to be? Better yet, what caused it to change? From its dark Voodoo origins to its modern viral form, in the last half-century the zombie has lumbered its way across the invisible boundary that separates superstition and science. Many would agree that the zombie symbolizes some of our most primal human fears. If this is the case, perhaps it is only natural that the zombie has changed along with our fears. Who knows what new terrors await us in the ages to come?

From Superstition to Science

In Chapter 1, we looked at the superstitious origins of the zombie, a body that is dead yet somehow reanimated. However, the modern zombie concept bears little resemblance to its "Voodoo zombie" predecessor. This evolution is not a rare occurrence, and it certainly isn't exclusive to zombies. Most fictional monsters (zombies, vampires, werewolves, and so on) had their beginnings in myth or superstition. As the group that created the monster advances, however, superstitions are gradually shed and replaced by new knowledge … but, for some reason, the monsters are not. Instead, the lore surrounding the monster in question is altered to match the new knowledge, thereby allowing it to remain frightening, sitting right on the edge of disbelief. After all, humans are not frightened by things that can be easily dismissed.

Consider, for example, the years of your early childhood. Many of the things that may have frightened you back then no longer hold any power over you now that you are older. Perhaps you were frightened that some kind of boogeyman or creature would come out from under your bed and drag you off to a realm of unknown horrors. Most kids share this kind of fear, in myriad versions. However, as children, we are frightened by such things because we *believe* that they are possible. As we grow up and our understanding of our environment advances, we come to recognize the impossibility of the thing we once feared. However, this does not mean that we altogether abandon our fear. As adults, we replace our childhood boogeyman with new (and sometimes just as unreasonable) objects of panic. The causes of our adult fear are not invisible murderers or monsters that emerge miraculously from a closet. They are instead often based on the very real threats that we discover as we venture out into the real world, which can be equally terrifying.

The Atomic Age and the Zombie

The world was forever changed on July 16, 1945, when the United States carried out its first test detonation of an atomic bomb (dubbed "Trinity") at the White Sands Missile Range near Las Cruces, New Mexico. This event officially launched the world into a period that was referred to in later years as the Atomic Age. The Trinity bomb was only the beginning. In less than a month, a powerful atomic bomb, dubbed "Little Boy," was dropped on the Japanese city of Hiroshima on August 6. Three days later, the even more powerful atomic bomb "Fat Man" was unleashed on Nagasaki in an attempt to secure the unconditional Japanese surrender that would end World War II.

Brains!

> The Atomic Age, as a historical period, is most commonly dated from the detonation of the first atomic bomb (July 16, 1945) to the fall of the Soviet Union in 1991. However, some historians argue that it began in 1942 with the hatching of the Manhattan Project. Also, some claim that it ended in October 1963 when the Partial Test Ban Treaty was signed, which forbade aboveground tests of nuclear weapons.

The introduction of the enormous power of the atom led to a diversity of public reactions, ranging from enthusiasm to sheer terror. To add to the confusion, no one knew for certain what the long-term repercussions would be for using this new technology. When medical and scientific investigations were carried out in the aftermaths of these two bombs, the outlook was grim. Tens of thousands of Japanese people had been killed in the blast (reduced to ash in half the time it takes a dropped spoon to hit the floor), and those who remained had been horribly injured. But scientists and doctors noted something odd regarding the injuries of survivors.

Many of the survivors had not been touched by the actual explosion (or any fire, for that matter), but were pouring in with mysterious and severe burns all over their bodies. Other people in the surrounding areas soon began to fall seriously ill, and it seemed as if their sickness was somehow linked to the bomb. Pregnant women experienced a wave of stillbirths, and many babies who survived had serious birth defects. Bombs had never before caused such things. What could burn a person without fire? How could a bomb make people sick and even detrimentally affect the health of unborn children? The answer to these questions introduced the world to a new and terrifying concept—radiation.

Needless to say, the feelings of stability and security that the atomic bomb was thought to instill in the American people did the exact opposite. Everyone in the world was scared to death of radiation. If radiation could cause sickness, stillbirths, physical deformities, mutations, and (as later discovered) various forms of cancer, what *other* horrors could it produce? This newfound, widespread fear of the atomic unknown soon became a dominating theme in the quickly growing realms of horror entertainment.

Brains!

As the Atomic Age progressed, the United States wasn't the only country with nuclear weapons for long: an arms race arose with Soviet Russia. Americans were terrified that the horrors unleashed on Hiroshima and Nagasaki might be repeated on their home soil. The U.S. government began a now infamous "duck and cover" campaign, in preparation for possible nuclear attacks, which consisted of emergency drills in which students and employees took cover under desks and tables while placing their arms over their heads (which, in reality, would have been absolutely *useless*). Today it's speculated that this campaign was meant to curb public fear more than to prepare for a real nuclear attack.

Radiation soon became the "nuclear boogeyman" of the Atomic Age and remained so well into the late 1980s (a decade marked by a flood of post-nuclear holocaust/world war/apocalypse films).

Suddenly, the fiction world was inundated with fantastical images depicting the hypothetical horrors of radiation—mutant animals, giant insects, apocalyptic wastelands, experiments gone wrong, and (of course) the walking dead. The presence of radiation-born monsters continued for decades. As Americans watched men venture into outer space, some of them worried that perhaps some even more terrible forms of radiation would be discovered. What if some kind of "space radiation" could somehow reanimate the dead? Zombies hit the entertainment mainstream with a vengeance, and a plethora of new films and short stories played out such scenarios. One of the most well-known portrayals of what some now refer to as the "Atomic Age zombie" is undoubtedly George A. Romero's landmark 1968 zombie film *Night of the Living Dead* (for more on Romero's films, see Chapter 10). This film suggested that its lumbering undead killers were spawned by a mysterious form of radiation brought to Earth by a returning unmanned spacecraft.

The cause wasn't the only thing new about the Atomic Age zombie. This new depiction of the walking dead included an additional, horrifying element—they ate living human flesh. Whereas the previous fictional zombies had indeed been creepy in their own right, they had never been shown attacking, murdering, and devouring the flesh of their screaming living victims. This flesh-eating element remains a central part of our modern zombie lore. In fact, one would be hard-pressed to find any fictional story about zombies that does not adhere to this theme.

> **Brains!**
>
> George A. Romero's 1968 classic *Night of the Living Dead* was the first zombie movie to depict zombies as having a physical cause (space radiation). All previous zombie fiction had depicted the walking dead as the result of Voodoo or some other kind of black magic.

The Viral Zombie

While people today still have a healthy level of fear and respect for radiation, it no longer holds the same power to frighten that it once did. Today humans have learned how to properly address and protect themselves from most forms of radiation. Also, decades passed in the Atomic Age with no unbelievably remarkable results. No giant spiders ... no mutant animals ... *no zombies.*

> **Moooooaaaaan...**
>
> Technically speaking, viruses are not independent living organisms. A virus is generally defined as a submicroscopic parasite that requires a living host in order to sustain its life. Since zombies are generally thought to be dead, more or less, it would seem that "zombie virus" would be a bit of a misnomer. Regardless, it would be hard to define the viral zombie any other way.

Even suggesting to someone in today's world that radiation might be capable of creating *anything*, especially something as incredible as reanimated corpses, would be regarded as ridiculous. This is mainly because it's become almost common knowledge that a strong amount of radiation most likely will harm, deform, or kill any life forms exposed to it—after all, it has never been shown to do anything else. So once again, the pseudo-superstitious myths surrounding radiation have been debunked and shed. The zombie, however, has remained. The boogey-man has changed his stripes to accommodate the fears of modern humanity.

So what scares us now? What invisible, terrifying force is capable of sending our technologically advanced society into a state of panic that borders on absolute pandemonium? You may have already guessed it—viruses. Never in human history has there been such an extreme and collective fear that some new or unidentified viral outbreak will wipe our entire species from the face of the planet.

Most Americans can still freshly remember the panicked weeks that followed the U.S. Center for Disease Control's ominous announcement that the H1N1 virus (commonly known as "swine flu") had jumped species from pigs to humans, meaning it could be passed from one species to the other. If the virus was not kept in check, news broadcasts said, the virus had the potential to make yet another jump that would allow it to pass from human to human. Most average people were previously unaware that such a thing was even possible. As with radiation, humans now are confronted with an invisible and potentially deadly force beyond our control. Adding to our panic is the fact that most of us nonvirologists don't really understand the specifics of how viruses evolve—so we don't know what they are capable of. We don't know, and fear of the unknown is one of the most basic phobias of the human mind. We're left asking a question that no one can really answer: "How bad is this going to get?"

The last few decades have been marked by the rise of several new—and sometimes very deadly—viruses, the most notable being the sudden (and still unexplained) appearance of HIV in the 1980s.

Many would agree that the virus has become the boogeyman of today. So perhaps it should not surprise us that today's zombies are depicted as being caused by a virus (sometimes manmade, sometimes not). It could be speculated that the Atomic Age's inclusion of zombies that bite living people is the origin of this addition to zombie lore. After all, it is common knowledge that most viruses can be passed through fluid transfer (which would certainly include a deep bite). And almost all zombie plots (including those in the Atomic Age) show that anyone who is bitten by a zombie soon dies ... and then comes back as yet another zombie who will attack and bite others, thus perpetuating the cycle. Further adding to the spooky factor of the "zombie virus" is the fact that it allows the zombies to exponentially increase their numbers in a very short period of time. Some zombie tales have portrayed planetary zombie takeovers occurring in only a matter of days.

Anyone Smell That?

Not convinced viruses cause general panic? Well, in 2003, a single teenager made a hoax website claiming an epidemic of Severe Acute Respiratory Syndrome (SARS) had swept Hong Kong so extremely that the government had closed its borders. The hoax sparked worldwide panic, sending thousands rushing to buy food (believing the border close would disrupt shipping avenues), and plunging global financial markets into chaos. The government of Hong Kong, in fact, had to officially announce that it was not closing the borders before the panic finally subsided.

The Brain Inclusion

One element that links all zombies together, whether said to be caused by Voodoo, radiation, or a virus, is the fact that they are all operating with compromised brains. Of course, as discussed in Chapter 1, Voodoo zombies are brain-damaged humans and are not actually dead. They do, however, retain at least a limited capacity for such human attributes as pain and emotion.

The radiation and viral zombies, on the other hand, are often shown as emotionless automatons. They cannot speak. They cannot reason. They can only seek out the living and attack. Zombies, as we now know them, are very single-minded organisms.

It is interesting to note that this neurological connection between the very real Voodoo zombies and

Brains!

A living human being's brain generally consumes about 20 percent of the body's available energy. However, this motivating organ only makes up roughly 2 percent of an average human's body weight (weighing around 8 pounds).

all fictional zombies, past and present, was made long before anyone had discovered (or even speculated) that Voodoo zombies were actually just the living, brain-damaged victims of a powerful neurotoxin.

Strength in Numbers

While most modern zombie depictions share a number of common elements, they are definitely not the same. Each zombie storyteller brings a unique spin on the zombie concept to the table. There are probably dozens of different fictional zombie types, if you get down to the minor details. For the most part, however, most of the modern zombie fiction and lore adheres to any one of the following primary formats:

♦ **The Voodoo zombie:** Since few of today's zombie-genre enthusiasts believe in Voodoo, this zombie type has come to be seen as completely obsolete (for details, see Chapter 1).

♦ **The "Night" zombie:** Named for *Night of the Living Dead*, anyone who dies will become a zombie whether or not they are bitten (getting bitten only causes the person to die faster). These zombies attack and eat any living, moving thing they come across, including humans, animals, and insects. For reasons unknown, they are afraid of fire. They are also extremely slow, weak, and clumsy. Destroying their brain kills them.

♦ **The Romero zombie:** Named after George A. Romero, these zombies were different from his initial "Night" zombies. Everyone who dies (bitten or not) still becomes a zombie, but the zombies do not fear fire (or anything, for that matter). They are still slow, weak, and clumsy. Destroying their brain kills them.

♦ **The "Return" zombie:** Named for the *Return of the Living Dead* series (see Chapter 12), these zombies are caused by a chemical spill. They cannot be killed, even by destroying their brains; they must be completely destroyed. These zombies also do not eat human flesh. Instead, and for unknown reasons, they eat human brains. These are also the only zombies in modern lore that are shown to retain their ability to speak. They may also be fast and agile at times, depending on their states of decay.

- **The "Sci-Fi" zombie:** These are the new breed of zombie, often caused by manmade viral experiments. They range from the usual rotting, undead corpses to frighteningly mutated creatures that are no longer recognizable as human. Brain shots still work against most of them. Sometimes they are weak and slow; other times they are strong and fast. It depends on the story or movie.

- **The "Fast/Rage" zombie:** These zombies are not always undead, but sometimes they are. What sets this group apart from the rest is that they are not at all slow, weak, or clumsy. In fact, they are fast and strong (which makes them a bit more intimidating). Some die-hard fans of the zombie genre do not agree with this zombie type, arguing that a reanimated corpse would destroy itself if it undertook such fast and extreme body movements. Then again, what part of the zombie concept are we supposed to believe?

In truth, there is not one generally accepted type of zombie. It is up to you to decide what you are willing to believe—well, at least, you can decide for yourself which kind of zombie you prefer. Some zombie fans say it's not important, and that it is the idea of the zombie apocalypse, and its effect on humankind, that is the most interesting. After all, zombie tales are not supposed to be about the zombies … they are supposed to be about us. The zombie has long been a popular medium for social commentary, as you will see in later chapters. Many zombie genre fans and filmmakers are fond of one thematic point—you don't make a zombie movie about *zombies*. You make a movie about *people* … and put zombies in it.

The Least You Need to Know

- The zombie depictions of the last half-century bear almost no resemblance to their Voodoo predecessor.

- During the Atomic Age, the walking dead were often depicted as the result of some strange form of radiation.

- Most modern zombies, sometimes called "viral zombies," are portrayed as the carriers of a lethal virus that reanimates an infected body after it expires.

♦ No matter what kind of zombie cause is being discussed, the one common element is the effect on the human brain.

♦ While most modern zombie depictions have shared elements, there are still a number of unique zombie types.

Chapter 3

The Extended Zombie Family

In This Chapter

- The undead *Chiang-Shih* of Chinese mythology
- The medieval European ghoul known as the revenant
- The undead *Draugar* of Icelandic lore
- The walking skeleton that the Great Lakes Chippewa call *Baykok*
- The zombielike, undead *Nachtzehrer* of Germany

Zombies aren't the only undead out there. In fact, all over the world there are tales of creatures that bear certain traits in common with zombies. That the dead will return to wreak havoc upon the living is an almost universal human fear, so it can be found in the folklore of almost every culture on Earth. These undead are not exactly *zombies* (at least, not as we think of them), but they certainly come close. The walking dead discussed in this chapter could be considered close relatives to the reanimated corpse we call the "zombie." They're like one big, happy, undead family. It's quite touching, isn't it?

Chiang-Shih (Chinese)

The Chinese creature known as the *Chiang-Shih* (sometimes spelled *Jiangshi*) is often referred to as the "Chinese vampire." However, it has more traits in common with zombies than it does with the usual depictions of vampires. In fact, the name *Chiang-Shih* means "hopping corpse." Like zombies, it does not initially possess any of the supernatural powers usually associated with vampires. The *Chiang-Shih* also share one other trait with modern zombies: they do not appear to retain any semblance of human intelligence once they have been reanimated.

According to Chinese lore, *Chiang-Shih* are the reanimated corpses of individuals whose souls, for whatever reasons, were not able to ascend to heaven after their deaths. This was often attributed to the manners in which they died. For example, suicide victims and executed criminals were often thought to be at high risk of being resurrected as *Chiang-Shih*.

The *Chiang-Shih* are called "hopping corpse" for a reason. They exhibit stiff and clumsy body movements, probably because of *rigor mortis,* a condition that causes a dead body's muscles and joints to stiffen about 12 to 24 hours after it has expired (depending on the environmental conditions). Because of their rigid body stiffness, they can only hop around instead of run as they pursue their victims. However, the rigor mortis does not seem to have any effect on a *Chiang-Shih*'s libido, and it is said that they will sexually assault any fair young maiden they happen to come across. *Chiang-Shih* are usually depicted as having long,

Moooooaaaaan...

The Chinese *Chiang-Shih* has a number of equivalents in other Asian cultures. In Japan, a similar creature exists called the *Kyonshi.*

Anyone Smell That?

It has been speculated by some that the original tales of the *Chiang-Shih* were spread by bandits and smugglers. The idea was that such tales would frighten law enforcement officials from disturbing them if they were ringing bells at night (which was said to be the main method for leading a *Chiang-Shih* back to its grave).

sharp, serrated teeth. A *Chiang-Shih* also has a long, pointed tongue and greenish skin (which is sometimes said to have a dull glow). The fingernails of a *Chiang-Shih* are long, thick, and sharp.

When they first reanimate, *Chiang-Shih* are a lot like pop culture zombies—weak, awkward, slow, and somewhat stupid. As time passes, however, they become stronger. Depending on how long it has managed to survive, a *Chiang-Shih* has the potential to become far more dangerous. This can be measured by observing how much of a *Chiang-Shih*'s hair has turned white. If only a little has turned white, it probably isn't too dangerous. If all of the hair has turned white, however, you should probably steer clear of it. A *Chiang-Shih* whose hair has turned totally white is commonly said to be able to fly and shape-shift (usually into a wolf). This also means that it undoubtedly possesses superhuman strength.

> **Brains!**
>
> In recent years, some Chinese filmmakers have begun to adopt the straighter, feline-like fangs of Western movie vampires in their depictions of *Chiang-Shih.*

Fighting the *Chiang-Shih*

How one protects oneself against an attacking *Chiang-Shih* is far different than how one would do combat with a zombie (for details on how to do that, see Chapter 15). It's a bit more complicated (and weird) than just shooting one in the head. For example, it is said that a *Chiang-Shih* cannot—or, at least, will not—cross a body of running water (such as a river). The lore claims that *Chiang-Shih* track their living human prey by the sound of their breathing (which suggests that they are visually blind, although no direct statements claim this). The lore claims that, because of this, simply holding your breath will render you invisible to an attacking *Chiang-Shih.* They are also said to hate garlic, just like Western vampires.

Almost all the lore about the *Chiang-Shih* claims that they are terrified of loud noises, especially anything that sounds like thunder. So you can usually scare one off by simply banging a couple pots together. The lore explains that this works because a direct hit from lightning (or even a very loud clap of thunder) is one of the few known ways to kill a

Chiang-Shih. They can also be killed if shot with a bullet from a firearm (which, interestingly enough, also works on normal people).

Brains!

> In ancient times, in both Europe and Asia, garlic was believed to have magical healing and protective properties. Modern science has shown that ancient people were at least correct about the healing part. Studies have shown that garlic has antiviral, antibacterial, and antifungal properties. In addition, chewing raw garlic sends a signal to the brain to begin producing *Allicin* (which is present in garlic), a powerful and naturally occurring antibiotic.

If you are dealing with a fairly new *Chiang-Shih,* meaning one that has little to no white hair, fighting it off is ridiculously easy. Some of the lore claims that this level of *Chiang-Shih* can be beaten back with nothing but a normal, everyday household broom. They also can't cross any border that has been made from a combination of rice, red peas, and iron filings. Once the *Chiang-Shih* has been subdued or killed, however, it has the potential to regenerate and come back. Therefore, Chinese lore claims that the body of a *Chiang-Shih* must be cremated immediately.

Best to Call in a Professional

If you are dealing with an older, high-level *Chiang-Shih,* such as one with mostly white or all-white hair, it is probably time to call in a professional. In most cases, this requires the services of a very unique type of *Tao* priest who is specially trained to handle this sort of thing (basically, slaying the undead).

Moooooaaaaan...

> **Tao,** pronounced "Dow," literally means "the way" or "the path." This is the Chinese root for the Japanese term *Do,* which also means "path" or "way." The Tao religion is based on searching for hidden cosmic truth and walking a righteous life path. Taoist priests dedicate their lives to serving good and combating evil. As a result, it is not all that surprising that they would also seek to combat evil monsters such as *Chiang-Shih* (no matter how insane that may sound).

These Tao "slayer priests" would bring with them multiple small slips of paper upon which were written prayers and magical inscriptions. Legend says these were written in blood or (more likely) red ink. The priest would then tack one or more of these slips of paper to the *Chiang-Shih*'s forehead (in movies, they are often shown throwing the papers in ways that defy the laws of physics). Once the paper hit the *Chiang-Shih*'s head, it would render the monster paralyzed and powerless. Once paralyzed, the priest would then ring a special bell that compelled the *Chiang-Shih* to hop its way back to its grave. The details are rather sketchy when it comes to what the priest would do after this. Some stories say the priest would kill the *Chiang-Shih* once it was back in its grave. Others claim that the priest used special prayers or magical incantations to ensure that the monster did not resurrect once again.

In some cases, certain *Chiang-Shih* survived too long, and so had become too powerful to be subdued with these paper inscriptions. They also could not be forced back into their graves with a bell. In such cases, the slayer priest had no choice but to engage the monster in one-on-one combat (and, according to most stories, these priests were *very* good with Kung Fu). This did not mean the priests went into the fight unarmed, of course. They often employed one of two special types of sword. The first (and definitely the most cool-looking) sword had a blade constructed of copper coins that were bound together with red string. Supposedly, a blade made in this way could inflict permanent wounds, meaning that a *Chiang-Shih* could not use its regenerative abilities to heal them. The second, less flashy type of weapon was simply a wooden sword that (much like the wooden stake in Western lore) usually had to be plunged into the *Chiang-Shih*'s heart to kill it (as you can imagine, wooden swords aren't that good for cutting off heads ... or cutting anything, for that matter).

Revenants (French/European)

The word *revenant* has its roots in the French term *revenir*, which means "to return" and literally translates as "one who returns." The implied meaning of just from *what* they have returned from (death), however, is far more important. Revenants certainly fall into the category of the undead, but they can be classified as neither zombies nor vampires.

Like zombies, revenants begin to suffer from decomposition once their corpses have reanimated. However, unlike zombies, the teeth of a revenant are said to undergo a certain level of deformity. Their teeth have lengthened, a trait similar to vampires. However, unlike a vampire's teeth, they do not grow as straight, sharp fangs; instead, they grow as terribly crooked and jagged dental protrusions.

Also like zombies, revenants usually stink to high heaven (likely from their state of decomposition). Some of the lore about revenants claims that humans can smell their foul stench from quite a distance, long before ever seeing them (even more so if standing downwind).

In medieval times, it was believed that revenants were the reanimated corpses of evil men, executed criminals, or those who died violently or due to the plague (especially those who succumbed to a fever). Back then, however, the lore did not yet say anything about revenants eating people or drinking their blood. It is commonly believed that the lore about revenants did not incorporate this additional element until sometime later.

Anyone Smell That?

Revenants may have been people mistakenly declared dead and then buried alive. A few "lucky" individuals may have managed to dig themselves out. Upon returning to their villages, however, their superstitious neighbors/relatives would have barred them from coming back home. This may have made them angry toward their neighbors, which explains why they were said to beat up anyone they encountered. The bites and scratches revenants reportedly had on their skin may have been inflicted in these scuffles. The spread of disease they supposedly caused may have been the result of others coming into close contact with the infected person (who probably hadn't washed since being buried, which explains the smell).

Revenants were said to carry out primarily physical attacks on the living and would attack anyone they came across. These attacks usually just consisted of savage beatings. In more extreme cases, the revenant would resort to biting, flesh eating, and blood sucking, usually infecting the victim with a mysterious and often fatal illness. Much like zombies, some of the early lore claims that revenants would intentionally bite or scratch their victims to create other revenants.

The *Draugar* (Norse)

The *Draugar* (singular form is *Draugr*) are living dead creatures that come from Old Norse legends. While the term later came to be used in reference to the undead in general, it originally had a more specific meaning. According to the available Norse myths about them, the *Draugar* are the living dead who venture from their tombs or graves by assuming the formlessness of smoke. Some stories say they are mariners who died at sea, reanimated after their corpses washed up on the shore (for this reason, they are sometimes depicted as having seaweed for hair or completely in place of their heads). In addition to their ability to change into smoke, *Draugar* can change their size at will, becoming as large or as small as they wish (though stories usually depict them doing the former). It is said they are easily detected by their stench, which is (as one would expect) the unmistakable scent of decomposing flesh. Their own flesh is usually described as being pale white, black, or putrid green in color.

Brains!

> The Norse people were the indigenous inhabitants of the regions that are now Norway, Sweden, Germany, Iceland, and other areas in and around Scandinavia. The Norse myths survive, but their religious traditions were for the most part lost when the land came under the control of Christian rulers.

After a *Draugr* has escaped from its place of rest, it will (much like a zombie) seek out and attack human victims. Some stories tell of *Draugar* that crushed people to death after growing to a gigantic size. In other cases, their suggested methods of killing victims are far more zombielike. For example, some stories tell of *Draugar* biting or eating the flesh of their victims. Sometimes they are said to drink the blood of a murdered corpse.

Most stories claim that *Draugar* cannot be killed by normal means. Some claim that weapons are useless against them. All insist that no mere mortal has the power to defeat one of these flesh-eating undead. In fact, most of the *Draugar* slain in Norse mythology fell only at the hands of gods or legendary warriors (which they usually achieved by dragging the unwilling undead back to their place of rest).

In the Norse tradition, certain steps would prevent someone from returning as a *Draugr*. The most popular method was to stab a pair of iron scissors into the chest cavity of a corpse before it was buried. Sometimes, perhaps in the absence of available scissors, a corpse's feet were bound (or their big toes lashed together with strong twine) and spikes or needles were driven through the bottoms (to prevent the dead individual from walking, if he or she resurrected).

Finally, there were methods for "confusing" the corpse. According to Norse belief, the dead could leave their place of rest only in the same direction they came in. Therefore, sometimes the coffin was turned in various directions before it was buried or was placed within a tomb, in hopes that the dead body wouldn't be able to find its way out. In cases of entombment, the body was taken in feet first and the inside of the tomb door was bricked up to match the walls before it was closed. It was believed that this would prevent the corpse from knowing the side where the door was located.

All this leads one to wonder, would people go through all this trouble unless they truly believed that the undead posed a valid threat?

"Bare Bones" *Baykok* (Ojibwa/Chippewa)

Stories of the *Baykok* come from the *Ojibwa* (also spelled *Ojibwe*, but more commonly referred to in the United States as the "Chippewa") tribe of the Great Lakes region. The word *Baykok* is often mistranslated as "skeleton," but it is more accurate to say that it translates as "skeletal/decomposed remains" or "skin-draped bones." The legend that tells of how the *Baykok* came to be still exists, although the origins are unknown.

Don't Get Bit!

Ojibwa became "Chippewa" in the Western pronunciation primarily because the initial O sound was not stressed by the native speakers and therefore went unnoticed by the Europeans who heard it spoken. As a result, European settlers would have heard Ojibwa as something like "uh-JEE-buh-WA," which they pronounced "Chippewa."

According to *Ojibwa* myths, the *Baykok* was once a skilled hunter of his tribe. One day, he came upon a large buck and began to pursue it. The animal eluded him time and again, but the hunter did not give up. After a long and difficult hunt, this hunter lost his target and his way. He wandered the woods for many days, unable to find his way back home. Eventually, the hunter reached the point of starvation and became too weak to continue.

Proud by nature, the hunter grew bitter about his situation and the fact that he would be deprived of living out the rest of his life. So with his dying breath, the hunter vowed that his spirit would never leave his body, even if it died (which it did). Later, his spirit was roused by a group of hunters who happened across his badly decomposed remains. The hunter arose as the *Baykok* and took his revenge. He attacked and devoured the men, overcome by the undead hunger for human flesh (some versions of the story say he ate their livers).

Unlike zombies, which usually seek out their prey fairly indiscriminately, the *Baykok* is very specific about his habits and targets. For example, he hunts only at night and attacks only people who are alone (which is odd, since his first victims were several hunters). Also according to legend, he attacks only hunters and warriors. For weapons, the *Baykok* wields invisible spirit arrows and a mighty club for bludgeoning. He uses these to incapacitate his victims before he eats their flesh (or livers).

The *Nachtzehrer*

The German word *Nachtzehrer* has two common translations, either "night waster" (although this one is often debated) or "night eater/chewer/gnawer" (which is more accepted in academic circles). Like the Chinese *Chiang-Shih* discussed earlier in this chapter, the *Nachtzehrer* is often called a "vampire" even though it has more traits in common with a zombie.

Basically, a *Nachtzehrer* is said to be the reanimated corpse of a person who has recently died, usually from an illness (especially if that illness later spread and proved fatal to others), suicide, violence, or any other unusual circumstances. Also, a male corpse that was buried too close to a woman who died during childbirth was said to be at risk for becoming a *Nachtzehrer*. In fact, some stories tell of *Nachtzehrer* being followed around by the reanimated corpses of these women.

According to most German stories, when a *Nachtzehrer* first reanimates, it is immediately overcome with such a terrible hunger that at first it gnaws upon parts of its own body. When this is no longer enough to satisfy them, they find a way to break free from their graves or tombs to seek out human victims upon which to feed.

German folklore offers a number of methods for preventing a potential *Nachtzehrer* from rising from its grave. The least extreme way of doing this is to place a coin or stone in the corpse's mouth or bind its jaw shut with a tightly knotted band of cloth (sometimes just tying it around the corpse's neck was said to be sufficient). It was also said that a piece of dirt (especially if from sanctified ground) could be placed under its chin.

The more extreme methods of dealing with a potential *Nachtzehrer* cover the usual bases one would expect when it comes to disposal of the undead—the first, of course, being the popular method of chopping off the head of the deceased. Another way was to hammer an iron spike through the head until it secured the body to the earth or coffin. Lastly, one could drive a nail through the corpse's tongue until it was pinned to the bottom of its mouth (apparently, it was thought that this would prevent them from wanting to eat).

The Least You Need to Know

- The zombie shares traits in common with many similar undead figures from cultures all over the globe.

- While the *Chiang-Shih* is often called the "Chinese vampire," it has more traits in common with zombies.

- In medieval Europe, revenants were believed to be the reanimated bodies of the recently deceased (though they may have just been mistaken for dead and buried alive).

- The *Baykok* certainly is not a zombie, but the shared traits are undeniable.

- The *Nachtzehrer* is also often called a "vampire," but from descriptions, it seems to bear a greater resemblance to a zombie.

Chapter 4

Psychology, Philosophy, and the Living Dead

In This Chapter

- The many reasons we fear, hate, and love zombies
- The virus phobia aspect of the modern zombie concept
- The conformity aspect of the modern zombie concept
- What zombies can tell us about human civilization
- The heavily debated concept known as the "philosophical zombie"

What is it about zombies? What makes them such a popular part of the modern horror genres? The presence of zombies, even hypothetically speaking, reflects all that is worst about human nature and modern civilization.

When it comes to the survival of the human race, zombies represent the worst-case scenario. They are very extreme representations of our modern fears about the threat of viral outbreaks: a virus that aggressively spreads and defies conventional methods of containment. They are a horde of mindless automatons, seeking to force us to join them. To make matters worse, there is a basic human acknowledgment that (hypothetically speaking, of course) the walking dead would outnumber the living well before anything could be done to stop them. Philosophically, zombies are organisms that act without any sense of consciousness (or conscience).

So the answer to why the modern understanding of zombies so profoundly affects us is that, ironically enough, they *are us*. At least, they are what we fear to become.

Why Do We Fear Zombies?

If you think about it much, a zombie isn't all that threatening. First of all, zombies do not possess any supernatural powers (unless you count being dead and walking around). In the majority of common modern depictions, a zombie is weak, slow, clumsy, and dumb as a rock. Against such an opponent, just about any able-bodied person could fight off a zombie without too much trouble. In fact, a fit, combat-trained individual could probably dispatch a group of four to six zombies fairly easily.

So, considering all of this, why are zombies so frightening? What makes them seem so dangerous?

The modern zombie is referred to by some as the "viral zombie," to differentiate it from the far different Haitian Vodun zombie. This zombie is frightening because, by human reasoning, the human race would not be faced with just one zombie. As the word *viral* suggests, one zombie quickly becomes a dozen zombies. And a dozen zombies can quickly multiply into hundreds of zombies.

The viral zombie frightens us because our human minds can hardly fathom surviving them, since it takes only one bite to become infected. Consider how quickly zombies would multiply. A risen zombie would bite its first victim, and then there would be two zombies. These two would go on to bite two more victims, bringing the count to four. Without immediate and appropriate human intervention, this exponential growth would continue unchecked. Soon the undead would outnumber the living. As you will see later in this chapter, there is even scientific/mathematical data to support this hypothesis.

One way to think about the threat posed by the concept of viral zombies is to consider ants. If a single ant is cornered by an animal or larger/stronger insect, it is likely to get squashed, eaten, or otherwise torn apart. So one ant is not very dangerous. A horde of ants, however, can overtake, kill, and consume far larger and stronger organisms, both insects and animals alike. In fact, in some regions of the world, ant hordes have killed and devoured large forms of livestock and even *human beings*, picking their bodies clean right down to the bone. Just like ants, the potential threat of the viral zombie concept increases as their numbers increase.

Brains!

Many zombie fans share the opinion that the downfall of the characters in George A. Romero's landmark zombie film *Night of the Living Dead* (for more information, see Chapter 10) was caused by their own efforts to secure the house in which they took shelter. The constant banging noises caused when they boarded up windows and barred doors, along with the use of fires to hold back advancing zombies, would have caught the attention of just about every zombie for miles around.

In addition to the threat of their numbers, viral zombies are commonly portrayed as being attracted by movement and sound. This further compounds the threat of their quickly increasing numbers. In fact, one could say that this is the greatest danger posed by viral zombies. Once a single zombie has detected and locked on to its living human target(s), it is commonly depicted as letting out a terrible wail or intense moan that immediately attracts all other zombies within earshot. Because of this, a person who is detected by one zombie will almost immediately become the target of dozens of zombies.

Many zombie films have played out such scenarios. Humans who have taken refuge in a home or other structure are at first found by no more than a few zombies. Within a day, however, the few have become a few dozen. Within a few days, the besieged humans find themselves surrounded by the living dead. This ability of viral zombies to call and assemble in vast numbers robs humans of any security that may come from the idea of fortified structures. The usefulness and security of structures and fortifications becomes nullified, no matter how well they are stocked, bricked over, boarded up, or otherwise supplied and reinforced. Surrounded by an army of walking corpses, such places would cease to be safe havens and would become little more than long-term death traps.

Zombies and Virus Phobias

The boogeyman never dies—he just changes his appearance. When it comes to monsters in general, the rationale surrounding zombies has changed drastically over the years. Most human beings no longer believe in superstitious causes, such as magical spells or Voodoo curses. This does not mean, however, that the human mind is without fear—far from it. The old superstitious fears have simply been replaced by new, more "rational" ones. For example, in the 1950s, people feared unknown repercussions from nuclear radiation (as discussed in Chapter 2). In today's world, this fear has subsided. Instead, the potential release and spread of some unknown and potentially catastrophic virus has become the new boogeyman of the age.

Think about the panic caused by the discovery of anthrax-laden envelopes that were delivered to members of the press and the American government. Consider the extreme steps that several world governments took in response to the new strain of the H1N1 viral strain, more commonly known as swine flu. The widespread panic and extreme responses caused by these recent cases most definitely pale in comparison to those that would likely be caused by an outbreak of a zombie virus. Why? Because a person infected with anthrax or H1N1 would soon be too ill to leave the house. If the person was aware that he was infected, he would most likely do everything in his power to keep from spreading it to others. A person infected with and reanimated by a zombie virus, however, would not behave in such a way. Instead, the zombie would get up and actively seek out the uninfected living in order to bite and infect them. As a result, the zombie virus would be a worst-case contagion, the likes of which the world has never seen.

Brains!

Few viruses are even close to 100 percent contagious (as the zombie virus is often portrayed to be), meaning that not everyone exposed to a virus becomes infected. Those viruses that are so highly contagious are also, lucky for us, rarely fatal and a case of infection often leads to increased resistance or immunity. Take, for example, the chickenpox virus. Almost all of us become infected with it as children. It makes an infected person ill, but most humans can only be infected with chickenpox once. Imagine, however, if the chickenpox (which is almost 100 percent contagious) was also fatal? It could have wiped out the human race quite a long time ago.

It is generally agreed that anyone who is bitten by a zombie will die and be reanimated. However, the general nature of infection varies from one zombie depiction to another. For the most part, there are three general schools of thought regarding how a zombie virus would behave.

♦ **Dormant infection only:** In this case, the virus spreads throughout the world and remains unnoticed until the recently dead begin to reanimate. In this case, everyone on the planet, bitten or not, will reanimate after death. In recent years, this depiction has become a bit of a rarity.

♦ **Active infection only:** This scenario suggests that only those who are bitten by a zombie will be infected and ultimately die as a result, only to reanimate after their deaths and infect others. However, in this depiction, those who die of natural causes or without having been bitten do not reanimate after death.

♦ **Dormant and active infection:** This integrates both of the previous scenarios. All persons who die will still reanimate. Those who are bitten by zombies will die much faster, but they will still reanimate soon afterward. This is a popular depiction of the zombie virus, mainly because it is the most frightening of all three. In the hypothetical case of a zombie virus outbreak, it couldn't get any worse than this.

Zombies, Individuality, and Conformity

As human beings, we like to view ourselves as a collective of unique individuals. In fact, you would likely consider it an insult if someone referred to you as a "follower" or "sheep"; such labels would imply that you are a person who does not think for yourself, but instead allows others to think for you. At the same time, however, all humans are aware of our natural tendency to act with a "mob mentality." Especially in the United States, we are a culture obsessed with our individuality, yet prone to conformity. This contradiction is in our face every day, yet we do our best to look away so that we can try to ignore this ugly reality of "conforming individualism" or "individualistic conformity."

Take, for example, one particular episode of the History Channel show called *Surviving History* (which regularly reconstructs torture machines and execution devices from humanity's darker past ages). In this episode, members of the show wanted to see what would happen if they put a living human being, bound in wooden *stocks*, in the open square of a public strip mall. They then provided a large bucket of tomatoes and encouraged people to throw them. At first, no one was willing to throw tomatoes at the man. When members of the show began throwing them, however, this attitude shifted almost immediately. Within 10 minutes, a long line of people (some of them even children and parents) were ready to throw tomatoes at a perfect stranger. Of course, this was done all in good fun, but it demonstrates an interesting point. People were willing to participate only when they saw that others were doing so. This is a perfect example of how the conformist side of human nature (which we openly detest in our words yet seem to prefer in our actions) influences our decisions and behaviors. We don't like the idea of "the mindless mob," yet it is in our nature to join it.

Mooooooaaaaan...

From premedieval to around colonial times, **stocks** were used as a punishment for minor criminal offenses (such as not paying a debt or petty theft). Their necks and wrists were clamped down in three tight-fitting voids between two pieces of heavy wood, attached by a hinge and secured by a lock. The person was left in public for the duration of the sentence. Such persons were "fair game," and often mobs entertained themselves by harassing the helpless person in various ways—spitting on them, throwing rotten food (or worse, stones) at their heads, and even beating them with sticks. Being bound, people in stocks couldn't dodge such attacks.

Sometimes humans fall into the trap of participating in conformist behavior under the mistaken belief that they are actually exercising their *individuality*. Think of how so many "rebellious" or "anarchist" teenagers rant against such indistinct things as "the system" and bemoan the "evils of corporate America." Yet many of these same teenagers then drive to the local mall and buy the latest trendy "punk" clothes, accessories, and hair dye at a chain store that is owned by a large corporation, a part of the very same "evil corporate system" they claim to be rebelling against. In fact, the idea of "dressing like a rebel" is counterintuitive, and such clothes may as well be uniforms, since they identify the wearer as belonging to a particular group. But still they wear them. Why?

In the 1978 classic zombie film *Dawn of the Dead*, the leading lady puts forth the open question of "What are they?" as she watches a mob of lumbering zombies bang on the doors of the shopping mall in which their group has taken shelter. One member of the group offers her the insightful answer, "They're us ... only dead." And, indeed, they are us. Many of the zombies clawing at the doors of the shopping mall wore the uniforms that both set them apart as individuals and made them a part of certain systems—a young man in a baseball uniform, his catcher's mitt still hanging from his hand; a mutilated woman in a bloody nurse's uniform; a middle-aged man in a disheveled suit and tie. They were all a shadow of living humans, but they no longer had the ability to consider the existential choice between conformity and individuality, or any of the countless possibilities in between.

The walking dead were mindless automatons, completely incapable of exerting any influence over how they behaved, nor did they even possess the necessary level of human consciousness to question *why* they behaved as they did. They no longer pondered the motivations for what they did … they just did it. This part of the fictional zombie concept, as we will see later in this chapter, has had a major impact on new concepts in mathematics, philosophy, and even computer programming.

We can try to ignore our own conformist tendencies, but zombies are not so easy to brush aside. They slap us in the face with this fact and are an extreme representation of human conformity. One zombie is fairly harmless; only through its role as a part of a collective does it become dangerous. Zombies are 100 percent single-minded in their actions. They exist only to bite and consume human flesh, in order to infect any remaining uninfected and thereby force them to become one with the collective. Once a person has been infected, dies, reanimates, and is assimilated into the zombie collective, the individual ceases to exist and becomes only a mindless servant to this collective's goal (or perhaps it would be better to call it a "nongoal," since zombies don't really have any conscious reasons for anything they do). Our collective would fall to their collective. Our land would become their land—the land of the dead and the home of the collective. This idea is horrifying even to consider.

Zombies, Weird Math, and Human Civilization

The zombie concept has an interesting paradox—zombies are an extreme representation of conformity, yet their presence would likely bring human civilization to its knees (if not just destroy it altogether). However, this is no longer just a point of speculation. That's right, there is now hard mathematical data to support the long-held assumption that zombies would be the end of human civilization as we know it.

Professor Robert J. Smith? (who, for reasons unknown, spells his last name with a question mark) and a joint team of mathematicians from both Ottawa University and Carleton University in Canada apparently felt that it was time to put the old hypothetical beliefs about the zombie threat to the ultimate test on a computer. They didn't just go the usual route of killing CGI'ed zombies in some generic first-person shooter game on an Xbox 360, however. Nay, they went above and beyond the call of duty, and the results of their research give some pretty bleak odds for human survival and the continuation of civilized societies all over the globe. They published their findings in an article entitled "When Zombies Attack!: Mathematical Modeling of an Outbreak of Zombie Infection," which has been included in the book *Infectious Disease Modeling Research Progress*. Despite the lengthy title, the world of zombie fandom is more than a little thrilled.

To create a proper model for a zombie virus outbreak, the mathematicians had to decide on certain variables. For example, would they go with slow- or fast-moving zombies? They chose the traditional, fairly slow zombie. Certain other factors could not be accurately addressed: for example, how effective would the average person be at identifying and killing a zombie? Basically, it was difficult to determine whether a certain percentage of people would identify the outbreak for what it was and respond appropriately (by attacking the brain or head of zombies). And if there was such a percentage of people in a given population, there was no readily available way to measure just what that numerical percentage might be.

Though based on a hypothetical and unlikely scenario, the model has very real applications. The motivation behind the creation of this model (aside from the fact that it is *awesome*) was to demonstrate how a flexible and adaptive formula can be created to uncover fairly accurate estimates in the case that, for example, an unidentified virus emerged (not necessarily just one that caused zombies). The details of how the team created its mathematical formulas are long, detailed, and rather difficult for just about anyone who is not a mathematician to understand. So let's forego a discussion of all the super-technical stuff and instead pose the one question that everyone really wants the answer to: what did they find out?

According to the results of the study, the only hope for any human civilization faced with a zombie virus outbreak would be a fast, appropriate, and aggressive response (and the faster and more aggressive, the better the odds for survival). They also discovered that taking a defensive stance (long a favored method of dealing with zombies) is *not* the way to go. Only an offensive military response, put into action within a given timeline, would be effective in containing and ultimately ending a zombie virus outbreak.

So just how long is the timeline for such a response to be effective? Well, this outcome varies depending on certain variables, such as population size, location, terrain, and available military and law enforcement. For example, a stereotypical urban city with a population of roughly 500,000 people would require an aggressive military response within three to eight days (depending on how aggressive the response and how well trained the specific city or country's military and police forces were and how many could be mobilized). After eight days, however, it would pretty much be guaranteed that the civilization could not bounce back. What few survivors remained would likely be trapped, and trying to leave the city would only get them killed. The dead would overtake the living. To put it simply—game over.

The team's results were able to address one other longstanding debate about the zombie virus concept: should zombies be captured or studied in order to attempt to find a cure? According to their research, *absolutely not*. The results showed that such a plan would only lead to higher levels of risk to uninfected members of the population. And in the end, the scenario almost never succeeded; it only put off the inevitable outbreak—or, worse, sometimes reintroduced the zombie virus into an area that had managed to contain the initial outbreak. Nothing good ever came from doing this. Again, the only responses that resulted in any positive outcomes (that is, in which civilization did not end) were aggressive and prompt extermination campaigns. So the best plan would be to put away the chains and break out the shotguns.

A Philosophical Zombie? ... Seriously?

Okay, first of all, a philosophical zombie is not what it sounds like. This is not a zombie who walks around quoting Socrates and Aristotle. In fact, philosophical zombies aren't exactly zombies at all—at least, not in the way you might think. They are not the walking dead. A philosophical zombie is a living, breathing organism.

The philosophical zombie (sometimes referred to by the shortened "p-zombie") is a hypothetical concept in the study of consciousness, as it applies to not only philosophy, but to computing as well (such as in the case of artificial intelligence). Basically, a philosophical zombie is a living human organism that exhibits behaviors as though it is conscious but is not. This can be a little confusing to grasp, so perhaps the following example will help.

Imagine that there exists an alternate world that is a 100 percent copy of this one, which one might call the "p-world." In that world, there is a perfect copy of you, the "p-zombie-you," which is identical to you in every way imaginable, right down to the last molecule. Right now, as you sit here reading this book, imagine that the p-zombie-you is also reading this book, on the same exact page, matching you word for word. The difference between the conscious, actual you and the non-conscious p-zombie-you is that you are capable of phenomenal experience. When you read this book, you react to it with certain behaviors (a chuckle, a grunt, and so on) according to how you experience it. The p-zombie-you will behave just as you do and will at least appear to react in just the same manner, but it cannot actually react to anything because it is capable only of behavior.

For example, let us say that when you make your coffee in the morning and take that first, eye-opening sip of morning brew, you are refreshed, sigh deeply, and say, "That is good coffee." You would be saying and doing this set of behaviors in response to your own conscious experience of drinking your coffee. You know what good coffee is like, because you can understand that it is not like bad coffee. And because of this ability to have conscious phenomenological experience, you react accordingly. The conscious-absent, p-zombie-you will drink the same coffee, breathe the same sigh, and say, "That's good coffee." However, it will do this only in response to you; it will not react to the coffee, or even consciously experience tasting the coffee. The p-zombie-you is also completely incapable of understanding what good coffee "is like" or "is not like." It is only a puppet being moved by another being's consciousness, one might say, but not by its own.

Many schools of philosophy (such as materialism, behaviorism, and physicalism) argue that philosophical zombies are purely hypothetical beings and are otherwise completely impossible because they could not exist within the set laws of nature and existence. However, many scholars who study the philosophy of the mind point to computers, which act according to instructional data and will perform or mimic a behavior if so programmed. By this rationale, a computer with artificial intelligence would be able to act in a way that resembled consciousness without actually having conscious experience. Then again, computers are not living organisms ... yet.

The Least You Need to Know

♦ Zombies represent all that is most ignoble and terrible about the human condition.

♦ The fear of zombies often stems from real human fears regarding unfamiliar or uncontrollable forces in our world.

♦ As superstition gave way to the nuclear age, zombies were depicted as caused by radiation; this shifted to viral causes as fears about radiation subsided and fears about viral outbreaks increased.

♦ Metaphorically speaking, zombies are a frightening metaphor for the inner struggle many humans have regarding the conflict of individuality with conformity.

♦ Robert J. Smith? and a Canada-based team of statisticians put the zombie virus outbreak scenario to the test and found that only prompt, aggressive extermination campaigns would be effective.

♦ Philosophical zombies are not the walking dead, but a philosophical concept of a living human organism that has no conscious experience.

Part 2

Zombie Literature and Comics

Zombies have been a part of the literary tradition for well over a century. The various ways in which they have been portrayed, however, has changed drastically. In literature, the body of zombie fiction has grown from obscurity and entered the mainstream. Zombies have become a staple of literature's horror fiction genre. In fact, the walking dead have been immortalized in the works of many legendary masters of the macabre, such as H. P. Lovecraft and Stephen King. In the growing world of graphic novels, zombies offer the backdrop for many of today's most riveting illustrated tales. They have even influenced modern poets and inspired parodies of such literary classics as *Pride and Prejudice*.

Chapter 5

Zombies in Early Literature

In This Chapter

Few things have such a provocative impact upon human emotions as the concept of death—or undeath. In the realm of horror literature, zombies have reigned supreme for nearly a century, and their popularity has only increased as years have passed. In early zombie literature, the cause of zombie reanimation often stemmed from the debate of just how far humans (namely, doctors and scientists) should go to prevent death. Should we try to bring people back from the dead? And, if we succeed, will we be able to deal with the possibly horrific consequences? Not all the works in this chapter are specifically about zombies, however. This chapter seeks to educate you on the works that have influenced the evolution of zombies in literature.

Frankenstein

Believe it or not, there is a longstanding debate between certain zombie enthusiasts regarding Mary Shelley's novel, *Frankenstein*. The debate is usually something along the lines of whether Dr. Frankenstein's creation can be classified as a "zombie." It really breaks down to what one considers to be the correct definition for zombie. One side of the debate claims that a *zombie* should be defined as a reanimated corpse, regardless of how that reanimation occurred. Following this definition, this group claims that Frankenstein's monster qualifies as a zombie. The other side of the debate claims that this is not so. This group defines *zombie* by either the original Voodoo definition (see Chapter 1) or the modern definition of a zombie as a corpse that is reanimated, by either a virus or radiation, and eats human flesh.

Brains!

Mary Shelley (maiden name Godwin) led an odd life for a nineteenth-century woman, especially in her love life. Her romance with Percy Shelley began during his marriage to Harriet Shelley. Harriet suffered from serious postpartum depression after her second child, so Percy ran off with Mary and her cousin Claire in 1814. They traveled across France until they ran out of money and were forced to return to England. Mary, however, had gotten pregnant (the child was premature and didn't survive). In 1816, overcome by depression and shame (Percy carried out a cruel libel campaign against her), Harriet killed herself. Percy and Mary got married almost immediately. Mary's cousin Claire also became pregnant out of wedlock, and the father is generally believed to have been Lord Byron.

Mary Shelley's *Frankenstein* was the first novel to approach the idea of human reanimation from a nonsuperstitious point of view. Impressively enough, Shelley began writing the novel in 1816, at only 18 years old, while spending a summer (some say due to financial woes stemming from her scandalous marriage to a man whose wife only recently had committed suicide) at the estate of family friend and famous writer/poet Lord Byron. As time progressed, Byron, Shelley, and the others at the estate began to experience cabin fever (basically, they were at each others' throats). So they decided that everyone would go to their respective rooms and write a scary story that they would then return and read to one another. The short story that Shelley wrote became the basis for what is her most famous literary work. She finished the novel a year later, in 1817.

The Modern Prometheus

Though Shelley's novel is usually referred to these days as simply *Frankenstein*, it was first published in 1818 under the longer title of *Frankenstein; or The Modern Prometheus*. Due to the general presence of sex discrimination, Shelley originally published the novel anonymously. Since the introduction to the work was composed by her husband, Percy Shelley, many readers assumed that he had written it (and there are some who now claim Percy Shelley wrote it in such a way as to suggest that this was the case). The book was revised (including many citations and notations from her father, political philosopher William Godwin) and republished in 1831. It would not be anonymous this time, and was printed with Mary Shelley's own name on the cover. Percy Shelley had drowned in a boating accident in 1822. This may have allowed Mary Shelley to feel free to finally publish under her own name. She also took out her late husband Percy's introduction from the 1818 manuscript and replaced it with one of her own.

Braioal

> The subtitle of Shelley's novel, *The Modern Prometheus*, refers to Greek myth. Prometheus stole fire from Zeus (who'd declared it solely for the gods) and gave it to the human race. Prometheus brought humans the element that spawned all technology, from tools to weaponry. But he paid a hefty price for this act. Zeus bound him to a rock where his liver was torn out by a giant eagle (or vulture) each day. Every night, his liver regenerated and his side healed. Prometheus suffered for ages, until he was rescued by Herakles (Hercules). Shelley calls Frankenstein the "modern Prometheus" because he, too, pays a price for "playing with fire," so to speak, and treading into the territory reserved for gods.

Most of Shelley's novel is told in the form of letters, journals, and various forms of correspondence. Much of the novel is made up of letters written by sea captain Robert Walton to his sister, which tells the tragic tale of Victor Frankenstein and his creation. Walton tells the story as it was told to him when Victor Frankenstein was a passenger on his vessel (after he was mysteriously found stranded at sea in the frigid waters of the Arctic Circle). So most of the story has already occurred and is told through recollections.

Brains!

Although nearly all of the film adaptations of *Frankenstein* show the creature being reanimated with the use of lightning or electricity, this is not what occurs in Shelley's novel. In fact, Shelley's story does not give many specific details regarding just how Victor Frankenstein brought his abomination to life. The only detail she offers is that Frankenstein had to make his creature larger than a normal human because of the difficulty involved in replicating the various complicated and miniscule components of the body.

We learn that Victor Frankenstein had once been a brilliant young scientist, born into a wealthy family. Obsessed with unlocking the secrets of life and death, Victor told of how he began a series of gruesome experiments by which he intended to reanimate the dead. In the end, however, he came to realize that bringing back the dead was impossible. Instead, he decided to manufacture a living body piece by piece (though how he accomplished this is not explained). When he finally succeeded, however, he realized that he had created nothing short of an abomination. His creature was gruesome in appearance, and in the beginning appeared clumsy and stupid. Victor was so traumatized by the sight of it that he tried to pretend it didn't exist (even as it stumbled around his apartment/lab). Victor finally fled his home, and when he returned, the creature was nowhere to be found. Victor explained to Captain Walton that he was relieved by this and prayed that his horrible creature would fade away like a bad dream. This did not turn out to be the case.

A Tragedy of Secrets

The creature's mental abilities evolved rapidly, allowing it to think and eventually to speak. The ability to think, however, also gave the creature the ability to figure out what had been done to him by Victor Frankenstein. He realized that he had been created by this man, only to be rejected by that same man shortly thereafter. Rejected by his creator, and after receiving cruel treatment from others due to his gruesome appearance and large size, the creature eventually is given refuge in the meager home of a blind man. After a year, the creature set his thoughts to revenge.

The creature carried out a vicious campaign of retribution. He first killed a young boy he encountered, William, after learning that he was a son of the Frankenstein family. He then snatched a necklace from the boy's neck and planted it on the family's trusted servant, Justine (who was treated like a member of the family), as she slept. Victor, who had been away in Scotland continuing his research, returned home to Geneva when he heard of William's death. He arrived just in time to watch Justine be wrongfully convicted of the boy's murder and exe-cuted. Despite the fact that Victor realized his creature was responsible, he was unable to confess to it in order to save Justine from her fate.

Victor had long been in love with his distant cousin, Elizabeth, and the two were soon to be married. They had all moved to England just before the wedding, hoping to escape the horrible memories of their recent family tragedies. The creature, however, followed them. He confronted Victor in person and explained that he would kill Elizabeth on their wedding night. The creature explained that there is one way for Victor to save the life of his beloved bride—he must die. If Victor died, the creature explained, he would forever abandon his vendetta. If not, he would continue to take the lives of everyone Victor held dear. To make matters worse, Victor continued his experiments, and he and a colleague, Clerval, were planning to create another creature. Victor's monster found Clerval and killed him before heading off to continue his bloody path of revenge.

Victor married Elizabeth despite his creation's threat, basically plan-ning to defend Elizabeth (he even prepared a pistol) and engage the monster in a fight to the death. He figured that either he would suc-ceed in killing his creation, thus being able to live in happiness with Elizabeth, or he would be killed by him, meaning that the creature would not harm anyone else. This is not exactly what one would call a "win-win" situation ... more like a "damned if you do, and damned if you don't" sort of situation. Victor worried that the sight of the monster would traumatize Elizabeth, so on their wedding night, he told her to stay in her own room. Unfortunately, his plan to fight went south when the creature killed Elizabeth in her room while Victor was waiting for him in the wedding chamber.

Brains!

Mary Shelley's horrifying vision of science gone terribly wrong likely influenced H. P. Lovecraft's classic, serialized horror story entitled *Herbert West: Reanimator,* which shares the similar theme of a brilliant young doctor who works to develop an injection that can reanimate the dead.

Creation vs. Creator

With nothing and no one left, Victor turned down his own path of vengeance. He had pursued the creature for months, eventually tracking it to the Arctic Circle. This is how he became stranded and was found by Captain Walton. The ending from here varies depending on which version of the manuscript one is reading. The 1818 version had a shorter ending than the 1831 version, and later versions have also been modified for various reasons. Basically, however, they follow a similar theme. Captain Walton told this part of the story from his own perspective, since he witnessed it. Victor Frankenstein died (either from illness or while battling the monster), and his creation, after justifying his revenge to Captain Walton, either disappeared into the sea or went off into the icy tundra.

H. P. Lovecraft's *Reanimator*

Legendary American horror author H. P. Lovecraft published the first installment of his serialized short story series, *Herbert West: Reanimator,* in the February 1922 (volume 1, number 1) issue of the amateur journal *Home Brew,* which was published by his close friend George Julian Houtain. The story continued its run in that publication for six total issues, until the final installment in July 1922 (volume 1, number 6). Most of Lovecraft's story of one brilliant young medical student's horrifying journey into death and resurrection is set in Miskatonic

University, a fictional institution that he used in some of his later works.

Lovecraft's *Reanimator* has had a large influence on later depictions of the reanimated undead. West's chemical injection was successful in reanimating the dead. However, his resurrected corpses came back from death wildly insane, uncontrollably savage, incapable of speech, and dangerously violent. Lovecraft's homicidal undead are undeniably similar to the murderous, cannibalistic zombies that George A. Romero depicted in his debut film, *Night of the Living Dead*, roughly 46 years later (for more on Romero and his films, see Chapter 10).

From the Dark

The first installment, "From the Dark," introduced the reader to Lovecraft's narrator, who remained anonymous throughout the series. We learn that the narrator was a medical school colleague of Herbert West. Despite the fact that Herbert West is not the narrator, he is undoubtedly the central character of the story. The narrator and West have gone separate ways, and only when West was out of his life did he come to grips with how truly insane his colleague must have been. We also learn that West has recently gone missing.

The narrator met West when they were first-year medical students. He admitted being fascinated by West's outside-of-the-box ways of thinking, especially by his unique theories regarding the human body. West approached the human body as a mechanic would approach a machine. He believed that if a specific chemical serum could be injected into a body at or near the exact moment of death, the brain could be returned to function.

West began his experiments on rats and other forms of rodents, but to no avail. His ultimate destination being human reanimation, West decided that human subjects were required. He brought the narrator in on the venture, and together they stole supplies from the university and turned an abandoned farmhouse into their makeshift laboratory. At first, they enlisted a group of poor black men to do their dirty work of bringing in fresh corpses from the local graveyards. However, these human subjects proved no more successful than the rodents. West decided that the corpses had been dead for too long or were of bad quality. The two men decided that they would have to start stealing the corpses themselves. They began keeping a close eye on the daily obituaries for potential subjects.

They finally saw an obituary for a local working-class gentleman who died in an accident earlier that morning. The man also had no family to speak of and would be buried in a potter's field. They snuck in, stole the corpse, and hurriedly took it back to their farmhouse laboratory. They injected it with West's serum, but it seemed to have no effect. They left the body in the room and went into the lab to prepare another injection. While they were doing this, a horrible scream pierced the air. In a panic, they rushed out of the farmhouse in fear. Somewhere in all of this, a gas lantern was knocked over and the farmhouse went up in flames (along with their stolen supplies).

The two men realized that the scream must have come from the corpse. It had reanimated! They assumed, however, that it had been reduced to ashes by the flames. The following day, they read about the fire in the paper. They also read a story about the corpse being stolen from the potter's field and found terribly mutilated, as if it had been torn apart by animals or hit with the edge of a spade. This baffled West and his assistant, because they had been careful not to harm the body when they dug it up.

The Plague-Daemon

In the second installment, "The Plague-Daemon," some time had passed since West and the narrator had their ill-fated first human experiment. Their work had been seriously hindered by no longer having the farmhouse as a lab. West tried to convince Dean Halsey of the university to allow him access to the bodies in cadaver storage at the school's dissection lab. But his request was denied. West, you see, was rather arrogant by nature, and Dean Halsey did not look upon him very well as a result.

West's fortune turned around, however, when an outbreak of typhoid fever hit the area. Physicians were suddenly in short supply, so West and the narrator were called in to assist the infected. West was suddenly up to his eyeballs in dead and dying people. He tried out his new serum on several patients, but the only reaction he got was that some of the bodies opened their eyes. Even Dean Halsey was infected by typhoid, and West stole his corpse as soon as he died. The narrator helped him take Halsey's body back to his room in a local boarding house. They injected him with West's most recent version of the reanimation serum. He reanimated, but things went downhill from there. He behaved like an animal—and a very violent one, at that. He attacked both West and the narrator, knocking both of them out cold in his frenzy before going on a bloody spree of mass murder and flesh eating. Halsey brutally killed 12 people before the police were able to restrain him. He was declared insane and committed to a sanitarium.

Six Shots by Midnight

By the third installment, "Six Shots by Midnight," a substantial amount of time had passed. West and the narrator graduated medical school and now practiced as full-fledged physicians. They went into private practice together and set up shop in the little burg of Bolton, New England. They acquired a piece of property right next to the town graveyard, allowing them easy access to freshly dead human bodies.

Don't Get Bit!

> You might note that not a single story has ever been told in which a person who ventured into the territory of cheating death did not meet with a terrible end. It is a basic human understanding that the dead are not meant to be brought back to life, and this theme has existed since the myths of ancient times.

West and the narrator soon found themselves a unique test subject, a local black prize fighter who had died from a head injury that he had received during an illegal back-alley street fight. The organizers of the fight were more than happy to let West and the narrator deal with the body's disposal, since they didn't want to be implicated in his death. They took the recently deceased body back to their lab and injected it with the most recent version of West's serum. But nothing happened, so they took the body to a secluded area and buried it.

A few days later, a child in town went missing. The mother of the missing child died from the shock. She was brought to Dr. West. When he couldn't save the woman's life, her husband attacked Dr. West in a fit of anger. At almost midnight that night, the two men were shocked from their slumber by a loud pounding on their back door. When they opened the door, they saw the dead boxer standing before them. He was covered in dirt from clawing his way out of the shallow grave they had buried him in. By the way, he also had the small arm of a child in his mouth; he apparently had attacked and devoured the boy who had gone missing. West dashed for his pistol and unloaded all six rounds on the reanimated corpse's face (hence the title of this installment).

The Screams of the Dead

The fourth installment, "The Screams of the Dead," again occurred some time after the previous one. The narrator returned to the lab after a vacation to find a perfectly preserved cadaver. During his absence, West had redirected his attention to creating a new serum that could preserve a corpse if injected shortly after death. It worked the moment it was put into the bloodstream, so the body remained exactly as it was at the moment of injection and completely halted decomposition.

The man on the table was a traveling salesman who had died of a heart attack, according to West, while he had been conducting a physical examination. West saw it as a perfect opportunity to test his new preservation injection. He had been waiting for the narrator's return so that he could be there for the reanimation. They injected the man with yet another revision of the serum. He slowly began to come to life, and at first he seemed rational, calm, and normal. Then, as one might expect, things went sour.

The man began to writhe and scream, as if in agonizing pain. As the serum wore off, he began to die once again (after all, the serum only reanimated the brain—it couldn't regenerate the damaged parts of the body). With his (second) dying breath, he revealed that he had not simply died during an exam. He had been murdered in cold blood by Herbert West.

The Horror from the Shadows

The fifth installment, "The Horror from the Shadows," occurred five years after the previous one. West had volunteered to serve as a physician in World War I, more out of his desire to gain access to bodies for his research than out of any sense of patriotic duty. His work had advanced considerably. He no longer restricted himself to whole bodies. He was testing his serum on individual (read: "severed") limbs—arms, legs, hands, and more. He believed that successfully reanimating these would prove his theory that the body is a complex organic machine.

West developed a relationship with his commanding officer and fellow combat medic, Major Eric Moreland Clapham-Lee. When the plane that Major Clapham-Lee was on got shot down, West and the narrator recovered his body and brought it back to the lab. The body was nearly decapitated, so West upgraded him to "completely decapitated" and preserved the head in a jar, immersing it in a vat of his embalming serum. He injected the torso with his serum, minus the severed head. The headless body reanimated violently, and the head began to scream from the jar. It was repeating the last few moments of the major's life, screaming "Jump, Ronald! For God's sake, jump!" (Ronald was the name of the pilot who had been flying the plane.) In a moment of absolutely horrible timing, the camp was hit with artillery at that exact moment. Their experiment was destroyed.

The Tomb-Legions

The sixth and final installment, "The Tomb-Legions," occurred one year after West's and the narrator's return from World War I. West has fallen deeply into madness at this point. He has moved out of the town, setting up in a secluded house, located near a system of ancient catacombs (and he created a direct tunnel to them from his house). One day, West opened the paper and read a very strange (but frighteningly familiar) story.

The story explained that a man with what appeared to be a head made of wax (Clapham-Lee) had laid siege at the sanitarium that still held Dean Halsey from the university. The strange mob (presumably all those West had reanimated) demanded that Halsey, who had been dubbed the "cannibal killer," be released. When the staff refused, they stormed the asylum and freed him by force. Realizing what was really going on, West went into a state of near catatonic shock. The narrator went to his aid, also seeing the truth in the news story.

Soon there came a knock at the door. The narrator answered to find a group of strange men outside. One of them handed him a box, and he gave it to West (who refused to open it). They both took the box to the basement and set it ablaze. Suddenly, the reanimated burst in through the catacombs that led to the house. They did not even bother with the narrator, but headed straight for West—the target of their vengeance. They pinned West down and began tearing out his intestines. Major Clapham-Lee cut off West's head. The vengeful undead then disappeared into the night with his remains. When the police arrived to inquire about West's whereabouts, the narrator kept his mouth shut. He feared that to disclose what he had witnessed would get him a one-way ticket to the insane asylum. The memories, however, would haunt him forever.

The Shape of Things to Come (H. G. Wells)

H. G. Wells's *The Shape of Things to Come* is seen by many as nearly prophetic. For example, it was published in 1933, yet Wells managed to accurately predict the coming of World War II. While the cause and duration of the war didn't follow the true events (his fictional war lasted until nearly 2106), many of the weapons and devices in the novel exist in the real world today. The story is not a "zombie book," per se, but it does have some bearing on later ideas related to zombie fiction.

Brains!

H. G. Wells adapted *The Shape of Things to Come* for the silver screen and wrote his own screenplay. The film was released in the United Kingdom in 1936, under the title *Things to Come*.

The world's armies found themselves at a stalemate, and one side resorted to viral warfare. They unleashed a "sleeping sickness" that soon spread across the planet, creating a pandemic like the world had never seen. The virus caused those who were infected to enter a permanent trancelike state. They wandered aimlessly, walking from place to place and spreading the infection until they died of infection or starvation (or were shot by uninfected people to prevent the spread). The disease brought all human civilization to its knees. Many people see these attributes as similar to a zombie virus outbreak.

The Least You Need to Know

◆ Though people debate whether Frankenstein's creature can be called a zombie, Shelley's story was the first to depict a reanimated body caused by science.

◆ Many modern film adaptations of *Frankenstein* show Victor Frankenstein using lightning or electricity to reanimate his creature. In the book, however, his methods are not specified.

◆ H. P. Lovecraft's *Herbert West: Reanimator* is the tragic story of the brilliant but mad Dr. Herbert West, who develops a serum to reanimate dead organisms.

◆ The "sleeping sickness" of H. G. Wells's *The Shape of Things to Come* does not reanimate the dead, but it bears a number of similarities to a zombie virus.

Zombies in Recent Literature

In This Chapter

Never in the history of literature have zombies had such an overwhelming presence. This is certainly the age of zombies in literature, and since 1990 the undead have begun to cross the genre boundary of horror fiction into other areas. Take, for instance, such works as *Pride and Prejudice and Zombies*, which updates a literary classic by resetting the story in the zombie apocalypse. Consider *Zombie Haiku*, which uses a zombie theme to offer a new spin on a classical form of Japanese poetry. It would appear that, in our written works at least, zombies will leave an indelible impression on the current literary time period—and their reign appears to have no immediate end in sight.

The *Book of the Dead* Anthologies

The first edition of the zombie horror anthology *Book of the Dead* was published in 1989. Compiling zombie-themed stories by various authors, the anthology was collaboratively edited by John Skipp and Craig Spector. The running theme of the anthology is that all of its stories are set in, inspired by, or somehow related to the zombie films of George A. Romero. This anthology brought together a number of highly regarded authors in the world of horror fiction (Stephen King, for example).

Three years later, a second edition of the anthology was released under the revised title *Still Dead: Book of the Dead 2*. This edition introduced readers to a new collection of writers. The same Romero-based theme remained, but with the stories organized in chronological order in relation to the initial outbreak, thereby creating a timeline for the imaginary zombie apocalypse. This one also offered a foreword by Tom Savini, who directed the 1990 remake of *Night of the Living Dead*.

The Demonic Zombies of Brian Keene

Written by Brian Keene, the zombie-themed horror novel *The Rising* was originally published in 2003 and was closely followed by its frightening sequel, *City of the Dead*, which went to print in 2005. *The Rising*, Keene's first novel, gained widespread attention when it won the 2003 Bram Stoker Award for Best First Novel.

The Rising kicks off shortly after something went horribly wrong with an advanced and secret scientific experiment involving a particle accelerator. The experiment unexpectedly tore a rift between our world and another dimension. A horde of demons crossed over into our dimension, immediately possessing and reanimating the bodies of the deceased. The zombie apocalypse thus began.

> **Brains!**
>
> Keene's novels are unlike most modern zombie stories, most of which depict the reanimated dead as the result of a virus. The zombies of Keene's novels, however, are the result of supernatural causes. This supernatural element has become a rarity in modern zombie tales.

The Rising

The main protagonist of Keene's story is a construction worker in West Virginia by the name of Jim Thurmond. When the world went mad, Jim took refuge in his bomb shelter. He had originally constructed the shelter at the turn of the century, in preparation for the infamous Y2K crash (a hypothetical worldwide computer crash that turned out to be nothing more than a hoax). From his shelter, Jim battled to hold out against the advancing undead. Most of them were his friends and neighbors, and he didn't want to harm them. What is most heartbreaking is the fact that one of the zombies was his recently deceased, pregnant wife.

This wife was Jim's second. He had a son, Danny, from his first marriage. Danny lived with his mother in New Jersey, and while trapped in his shelter Jim worried greatly about his boy's welfare. With no word from Danny, and haunted by the fresh vision of his reanimated and pregnant wife, Jim found himself pushed to his mental limits. He even began to contemplate suicide. When his cell phone rang with a message from Danny, however, he abandoned his thoughts of ending his own life.

In the message, Danny whisperingly explained that he and his mother were in the same situation. They had found a safe place to hide from the zombies, but they didn't know how long it would be until they were discovered. Jim refocused his energy, stopped feeling sorry for himself, got his head together, and began to construct a plan to save Danny and his mother. Jim packed all the supplies and weapons he could carry and left his shelter. He planned to travel hundreds of miles, from West Virginia to New Jersey, across what had become an entirely zombie-infested country.

But first Jim had to come to grips with the fact that the zombies outside were not his neighbors, not his wife. He had to fight his way through them, and kill them if necessary. The zombies of this world were possessed by intelligent demons who reveled in the suffering of human beings. The possessed corpse of his wife even tried to mess with his head in a most gruesome fashion, by dangling his unborn child in front of him. This was only the beginning of the horrors in store for Jim. He soon learned that these were not the zombies from the movies. They could think and perform complicated tasks, which meant that they could drive vehicles, use weapons (including firearms), and even organize ambushes.

As Jim fought his way across the horror show that the United States had become, a scientist named Baker from the particle collider experiment that had unleashed the demonic zombies awakened to find himself a prisoner in his own laboratory. The demons had gone, but the pandemonium outside made leaving the underground facility impossible. He could not even venture outside the room, as one of his possessed undead colleagues lingered beyond the door. Ever the inquisitive scientist, Baker started up a dialogue with the demonic zombie.

As Jim traveled, he met an old black minister by the name of Martin. Knowing they had a better chance at surviving together, Martin agreed to help Jim reach his son in New Jersey. They were beset by dangers at every turn—zombified animals, ambushing gangs of zombies, and even other humans. They came across a father and son who were hiding together, and the two briefly traveled with them. The state of things, however, soon became too much for them, resulting in a double suicide.

Jim and Martin later met up with a prostitute and former heroin addict named Frankie. She had narrowly escaped from the madness of a National Guard unit who, under the leadership of a violent commanding officer, had taken to forcibly drafting men and forcing women into sexual slavery. With the help of a goodhearted private named Skip, she had managed to escape. The unusual trio—a construction worker, a minister, and a prostitute/reformed drug addict—continued on to New Jersey.

City of the Dead

City of the Dead begins with Jim finally locating his son Danny in New Jersey. Thankfully, he was alive. Unfortunately, the local gangs of zombies immediately surrounded the house and started forcing their way inside. The entire group—Jim and Danny, as well as Martin and Frankie—soon found themselves trapped in the attic. The zombies, unable to get to the attic, set the house on fire. As the house became engulfed in flames, they looked through a small window and saw Danny's neighbor, Don. He had taken refuge in his home's panic room. Using a ladder, they created a rickety makeshift bridge between the houses. They all made it across but Frankie, who tumbled from the ladder and came crashing down into a swimming pool.

In the panic room, the four men decided that their best chance of survival was trying to make a run for Don's vehicle. His Ford Explorer was sitting gassed and ready to go in the garage. As they burst through the garage door and into the street, they saw Frankie fighting desperately against the zombies in the front yard. She was badly injured from her tumble into the shallow swimming pool, and the zombies shot her multiple times. The men managed to get Frankie into the vehicle just as she went into shock and lost consciousness.

In order to keep spoilers to a minimum, if you want to know the rest of the story, you will have to read Keene's series for yourself.

World War Z and the Zombie Survival Guide

Max Brooks first released his best-selling *Zombie Survival Guide* in 2003 as a precursor to the post-zombie-apocalypse novel *World War Z*. Brooks followed this plan with the idea that he would first create a guide by which to survive in a zombie world, and then follow up by writing a full-length story based on the guidelines he had set down in it.

Interestingly enough, Brooks's story in *World War Z* does not take place during the apocalypse. It is instead written in the form of a chronicle, narrating the experiences of those who survived "Z-Day," as conveyed to the writer/narrator of the book. The novel reads much like a documentary, or perhaps a piece of creative nonfiction. This gives the book a somewhat authentic feel, even though it is clearly labeled as a work of fiction.

Brains!

Max Brooks is the son of comedic producer/writer/actor/director Mel Brooks, the creator of such classic comedy films as *Blazing Saddles, History of the World Part I,* and *Spaceballs.*

According to Brooks's story, the origins of the zombie outbreak were not concretely known. However, it was often suggested that the plague first began somewhere in China. The Chinese government did its best to contain the virus, but it did nothing to warn other countries of the incident. However, a number of infected Chinese refugees soon made their way to other countries. In addition, a thriving black market organ trade caused a number of organs infected by *solanum* (Brooks's name for the zombie virus) to be sold overseas. The result was a worldwide pandemic of the *solanum* virus. When an outbreak was reported in Cape Town, South Africa, the world was finally alerted to what was going on. For a time, the unidentified virus was mistakenly referred to as "African rabies." The madness and biting of those infected was mistaken for extreme symptoms associated with rabies, so at first a new strain of the rabies virus was blamed for the situation in South Africa. Soon, however, the truth of the *solanum* virus was revealed.

The infection began to spread rapidly, as only a handful of countries immediately initiated quarantine procedures, among them Israel. The United States dropped the ball more than anyone, and the American people were misled into a false sense of security when a vaccine for the zombie virus, Phalanx, was suddenly produced and released by a large pharmaceutical company. So the U.S. government did next to nothing to prepare for the spread of the virus, aside from the widespread distribution of the Phalanx vaccine. There was just one significant problem with Phalanx—it didn't actually work. By the time anyone realized their mistakes, the undead were everywhere.

The cities of New York and Yonkers were hardest hit during the initial days of the outbreak, turning the streets of these heavily populated cities into absolute bedlam. The U.S. Army was deployed to restore order, but the forces were soon turned back by a flood of reanimated corpses. The book refers to these days of chaos as the "Great Panic." Many people on the North American continent tried to flee the populated areas for the rural forests of Canada. However, a majority starved or froze to death because they were unprepared and untrained for such an existence. The United States and Canada may have taken a serious beating during the Great Panic, but Brooks showed that few other countries fared any better.

Iran resorted to extreme measures to prevent infected refugees from crossing over the border from neighboring India, destroying any bridges that connected the countries. The islands of Japan were overrun to such a degree that the entire uninfected population (what little remained, anyway) had to be evacuated to South Korea and other nearby countries. Many people abandoned land altogether and took to living on the sea, where the undead were unlikely to follow.

In reading Brooks's "survivor" accounts, we realize that the zombie outbreak brought human civilization right to the brink of oblivion. For a time, the entire United States east of the Rocky Mountains was lost to the zombie hordes. In fact, the book explains that it had been 10 years since the outbreak, and that only now have things begun to return to any semblance of the normalcy of the pre-zombie world. The undead were not yet completely wiped out. However, there were few enough of them that humans could once again return to living out their day-to-day lives in the open.

The world 10 years after the zombie outbreak was far different than the one we know. North Korea had become a ghost town, its entire population living in subterranean shelters. Russia had become a theocracy. Cuba was a democracy and had become one of the world's richest economic entities. China was no longer experiencing an overpopulation problem (since the outbreak had killed off millions) and had also become a democracy. More than ever, the United Nations (UN) had become a force to be reckoned with. The new UN was tasked primarily with eradicating the remaining zombies on the planet.

Dying to Live: A Novel of Life Among the Undead

Kim Paffenroth's *Dying to Live: A Novel of Life Among the Undead* was first published in April 2007 by Permuted Press. This post-zombie-apocalyptic tale is one of both despair and hope, and of the human drive to survive chaos and rebuild order against all odds.

The main protagonist of Paffenroth's story is a man named Jonah Caine, who managed to survive the worst days of the zombie apocalypse. As he wandered what is now a quiet, dead planet, Jonah sought to find some kind of meaning to it all. More than that, he wished to find some purpose to his bleak existence, and to find some sense to all the horrific atrocities that now saturate his world.

After months of aimless drifting, Jonah began to think that perhaps he was the only living human being left on Earth. However, he then happened upon a small band of survivors, led by an aging but capable military veteran named Jack. Guiding their way was a strange fellow named Milton, who seemed to have the vision of a prophet ... as well as an uncanny ability to exercise a certain level of control over zombies.

Jonah allied himself with Jack and Milton, and together they chose to adopt a new purpose, and to dedicate themselves to a great and noble cause—to create a community of living human beings and establish a foothold for humanity. In doing so, they hoped to rebuild both the human race, and some semblance of civilization that would be a foundation upon which they might one day grow strong enough to begin retaking the zombie infested planet.

Unfortunately, not all human survivors shared the idealism of Jonah, Jack, and Milton. The group members soon found themselves under siege not from the living dead, but from a marauding band of human survivors who used the lawlessness of this post-apocalyptic world to their advantage.

Dead World Series

The first installment of the three-part series *Dead World*, entitled *Dead Come Home*, is the collaborative project of authors Robert Anthony Fox and Nathan Robert Brown. *Dead Come Home* was released in September 2009 and made available exclusively at online booksellers. Set in the modern day, the storyline of *Dead Come Home* narrates the implosion of human civilization during the initial outbreak of the zombie virus. The novel does not seek to identify any specific cause of the virus, going only so far as to show readers where the "first zombie" comes from.

Dead Come Home is very character centered, as most zombie stories are, and follows the exploits of three main protagonists. The first is Mike, a young man in the process of returning home after completing a combat tour in the U.S. Marines as a Force Recon grunt. His arrival in the town he left behind so long ago was not the homecoming he had expected. Eventually, Mike's battle to stay alive put him on the same path as a young business intern named Joseph, who had fled the chaos of Dallas and became stranded in the small city of Wichita Falls. The two embarked on a westward journey, planning to rendezvous with an old military buddy of Mike's, courier and entrepreneur Hansel Hanse, at his safehouse in the Arizona desert. The landscape grew increasing volatile, however, and their group started to take on more members, further slowing them down.

As Mike and Joseph made their way toward Arizona, a young aspiring musician in Seattle named Lily was in her own fight for survival. Her parents, who ran a diner in a small Texas town, were unable to reach her. She had no choice but to attempt to venture halfway across the country to reach the relative safety of home. Like Mike and Joseph, however, she learned that this was easier said than done.

Pride and Prejudice ... and Zombies

Pride and Prejudice and Zombies is a parody written by Seth Grahame-Smith. The story follows the same plot of the original Jane Austen novel, but with one very odd twist. Grahame-Smith's parody takes place in an alternate reality of nineteenth-century England in which zombies are a constant threat.

Grahame-Smith is even linguistically savvy in his work. Since the term *zombie* did not enter the English language until the late nineteenth century (after Austen's story takes place), he does not use the term whatsoever. Instead, the zombies are referred to by alternate terms such as the "unmentionables" or the "sorry stricken."

The story obviously carries some new elements that are absent from the original Austen story. For example, the male characters often evaluate one another's zombie-killing skills. The female characters sometimes discuss whether they should carry a firearm, debating the fact that it is useful for protection against the undead but rather unladylike.

The Bennet sisters are still headstrong and intelligent. However, the education they received from their father included elements such as marksmanship and martial arts training. When the Bennet sisters were sent to attend the housewarming party of the recently moved in Mr. Bingley, they ended up having to defend the other guests from a sudden attack by the living dead.

Star Wars: Death Troopers

Like zombie stories? Yes. Like *Star Wars?* Yes. Then do we have a book for you! That's right: the living dead have finally spread to the galaxy far, far away with Joe Schreiber's *Star Wars: Death Troopers*. Published in October 2009, this book marked a new frontier for the literature of the *Star Wars* universe. While these books have always had a fair share of light saber violence (frequently ending with someone's hands getting chopped off), they have never ventured into the realm of what one would call "graphic violence" or "gore." This book changed all that. After all, what's a zombie story without graphic violence and gore? Well ... it's a bunch of moaning dead guys stumbling around like a gaggle of lost drunks. And that's just no fun for anybody.

Analos!

On September 10, 2009, a series of letters were posted separately on six official *Star Wars* fan sites, as well as www.deathtroopers.com, with the title *Death Troopers: Recovered Messages from Purge*. The letters were made up of nine total messages, one released each week and on a different site that fans had to search for. These were supposedly the transmissions sent by the Storm Troopers deployed to Dathomir in the original novel. In order to see all the messages, fans had to explore all six sites at least once.

Star Wars: Death Troopers is set during the time when the galaxy was still under the tyrannical rule of Palpatine's Galactic Empire. For reasons unknown to the Storm Troopers, a large contingent of them was sent to a rural location on the distant planet of Dathomir. The Empire had released orders to all civilian craft that they were to avoid the planet at all costs. The Storm Troopers heard rumors that the Empire was attempting to contain an outbreak of some kind of experimental biological weapon.

The soldiers arrived at a rural Imperial outpost called *Purge* to find it in shambles and apparently abandoned by anyone alive. Blood and bodies littered the place. Soon enough, however, the Storm Troopers learned the terrible truth about what happened in this place. As their dead comrades arose from their supposedly eternal slumbers, the Troopers found themselves surrounded and outnumbered. Would they be able to cleanse the planet of their infected, undead brothers in arms? Better yet, would they even make it through the night?

Zombie Haiku

Zombie Haiku, by Ryan Mecum, offers an interesting spin on zombie literature. The book is presented in the form of a blood-spattered, worn-out journal. The book is introduced by the gentleman who found it, and he explains that he knows little about the original owner (before he was infected with the zombie virus), except for the fact that he was a poet. He submits the poems to the reader as an account of humanity's darkest days, and the book offers a glimpse into the deteriorating mind of an individual infected with the zombie virus.

Mooooaaaaan...

A **haiku** is a form of Japanese poetry that is popular among the Samurai warrior class and Zen Buddhism adherents. A haiku is exactly three lines long, with an alternate 5-7-5 syllable structure. The subjects of haiku are often nature related, experiential, or both.

As the poet's brain began to fall increasingly under the influence of the zombie virus, he continued writing haiku poems. These poems give the reader an eerie glimpse into an infected individual's final moments of clarity, as well as the maddening hunger that follows. For example, one haiku that is written after the man has turned reads:

A man starts yelling
"When there's no more room in hell ..."
but then we eat him.

Some of the poems even address the various problems encountered by the living dead, such as decomposition and even damaged teeth. Take the following excerpt for example:

Always be careful
when you're biting teeth with teeth.
Dead teeth tend to lose.

Readers also get sickening portrayals of the voracious human flesh consumption that the infected zombie-poet carries out. He even goes so far as to write one haiku that would seem to suggest a sense of etiquette among the living dead:

The two of us take turns.
I chew when he bites and tears.
When I bite, he chews.

Don't Get Bit!

Don't confuse *Zombie Haiku* with its follow-up book, which was also written by Ryan Mecum, entitled *Vampire Haiku*.

The book is well illustrated, giving it the look and feel of a lost journal that really adds to the mood of the experience. Some have gone so far as to label it a "graphic novel," but this is somewhat of a misnomer. *Zombie Haiku* may have illustrations, but these do not depict the story itself. The story of the zombie poet is told through the written form of haiku, and while the illustrations might add to the book's effect, they do not directly depict the events of his final moments.

The Least You Need to Know

◆ The *Book of the Dead* anthologies are collections of zombie/Romero–themed horror stories by various authors.

◆ Brian Keene's novels are unique, in that his zombies are caused by supernatural instead of viral means.

◆ Max Brooks's 2003 *Zombie Survival Guide* is meant to be a framework for his 2006 post-zombie-apocalypse novel *World War Z*.

◆ *Dead Come Home*, released in September 2009, is the first installment of what is scheduled to be a three-part *Dead World* series.

◆ Books such as *Pride and Prejudice and Zombies* and *Zombie Haiku* use zombies to put new spins on classical literary and poetic styles.

Chapter 7

Zombies in Comics

In This Chapter

- ◆ Portrayals of zombies in comics, graphic novels, and manga
- ◆ The *Marvel Zombies* series, which portrayed zombified superheroes
- ◆ *Deadworld* zombies that are intelligent and organized
- ◆ *Escape of the Dead*, a direct sequel to *Night of the Living Dead*
- ◆ The Voodoo-zombie graphic novel, *War on Flesh*
- ◆ *High School of the Dead*, a popular zombie-themed manga

From major comic book labels like Marvel and DC to small independent publishers, zombies have all but taken over the comic book scene these days. From the United States to Europe to Japan, the undead have overrun the illustrated world of Western comic books, Japanese manga, and international graphic novels. There are now alternate zombie universes, zombie virus–infected superheroes, and even stories depicting intelligent races of zombies who invade the human world from some alternate dimension. Giving a proper treatment of all currently available zombie comics would require its own book. This chapter represents only a sampling of the zombie-related comic storylines out there.

Marvel Zombies

The widely popular *Marvel Zombies* series is probably one of the most chaotic and wild storylines ever undertaken in the world of comics. Involving dozens of characters across multiple universes, *Marvel Zombies* really takes a bite out of the traditional take on superheroes.

The original *Marvel Zombies* story was a five-issue series that was published by Marvel Comics between December 2005 and April 2006. The story was written by Robert Kirkman, with art by Sean Phillips. The covers were created by Arthur Suydam. Due in large part to the overwhelming popularity of the first *Marvel Zombies* story, a number of related storylines have been developed since. The very first *Marvel Zombies* story (and much of the related stories) occurs in an alternate universe of the Marvel Comics' world, called the *Ultimate* universe, which stars differing versions of Marvel heroes (for example, in the *Ultimate* universe, Captain America is referred to as Colonel America). The first appearance of the *Marvel Zombies* took place in *Ultimate Fantastic Four*, issues 21 through 23, in 2005. They then appeared again in *Ultimate Fantastic Four*, issues 30 to 32, in 2006. The entire series was later compiled into a graphic novel format, and soon after this, *Time* magazine awarded it the title of one of the top 10 graphic novels of all time.

In this alternate universe that also takes place in 2149, a zombie virus has infected the superheroes of Earth. Because of their superpowers, they have retained most of their cognitive abilities. However, their superpowers didn't give them immunity to the urges of undeath—like the urge to devour human flesh. Needless to say, superpowered zombies are not good news for the human race. Soon the whole world has been devoured and, in a hunger-fueled frenzy, the zombie superheroes turned on one another. At this point, things went nuts.

Magneto (a villain from the *X-Men* comic books) showed up on Earth, one of the few superpowered beings not yet infected. Unfortunately, the infected heroes ganged up on him, killed him, and ate him. After this, the intergalactic hero known as the Silver Surfer appeared on the planet and tried to tell the zombies that his boss, a galactic overlord named Galactus, was on his way to devour the infected planet and rid the universe of the zombie plague. After his speech, the gang of zombie superheroes—Colonel America, Spider-Man, Giant-Man, the Hulk, Wolverine, and Iron Man—attacked, killed, and ate him. To make matters worse, eating the Silver Surfer's flesh endowed those zombie superheroes with even greater powers. The group that ate the Silver Surfer then turned on the other zombie heroes and killed them all, thus wiping out much of their competition for food.

Galactus showed up to destroy the planet, just as the Silver Surfer foretold. However, he met with some opposition from the zombie heroes. Though they were fairly easy for him to hold off at first, the zombies put their heads together and created a device that amped up the powers they received from eating the Silver Surfer. With this, they managed to at least put a hurt on Galactus. Before they could finish him off, however, a group of zombie-infected supervillains showed up, and the whole scene turned into a battle royale. The infected superheroes were victorious and proceeded to eat Galactus. They absorbed even more cosmic power, just as they did when they had eaten the Silver Surfer. In search of food, the superhero zombies left Earth.

Deadworld Series

Deadworld was first created by Stuart Kerr and Ralph Griffin in 1987, with art by Vince Locke. The series was originally released by the independent comic book label Arrow Comics, and is now considered a cult classic by both zombie and comic book fans. Eventually, as happens to many independent comic houses, Arrow Comics went under and cancelled all of its titles. However, it handed the story of *Deadworld* to Gary Reed of Caliber Comics and sold the rights to artist Vince Locke.

Brains!

Deadworld has been considered for movie adaptations multiple times, but things have never panned out. After briefly being considered by Maysville Pictures, talks with several production companies are said to now be in progress, but nothing concrete has been announced.

Gary Reed took up the writing of the storyline, and Locke continued on as the series' artist. The first volume of the storyline was finally completed and released in 1992. The second volume began in 1993 but was stopped after only 15 issues.

In 2005, the story was picked back up by Image Comics, again with Gary Reed as the writer and Vince Locke as the artist. However, Image replaced Locke by issue #5 with new artist Dalibor Talajic.

Grølds!

> *Deadworld* is unique among zombie stories, in that it depicts a class of intelligent and organized zombies. Unlike the usual zombies, which attack the living without thought or cause, the zombies of *Deadworld* did so with a specific goal in mind: taking over the planet.

When a gate is opened between our world and a supernatural realm, a zombie plague is unleashed upon Earth. The dead rise from their slumber and attack the living. However, the zombies of *Deadworld* are not like the zombies we are used to. The zombies of *Deadworld* are led by an intelligent, ruling class of leader undead who passed into our world through the gate. At the head of the leadership class is King Zombie, a Harley-Davidson-riding, cynical, smart-mouthed character who enjoys tormenting the living and has his sights on world domination.

Zombies!

The *Zombies!* comic book series is a product of IDW Publishing. The storyline is broken up into three main parts: *Feast*, *Eclipse of the Undead*, and *Hunters*. The stories follow the tradition of Romero's films, in that they are very character centered. The series adheres to the number one rule of good zombie storytelling—they are not stories about zombies, but stories about human beings (dealing with zombies).

Zombies! Feast

Feast is the first major part of the *Zombies!* comic book series. It is set during the initial outbreak of the zombie virus. While zombies were running rampant, murdering and feeding on the living, the walking dead were not the only problem. In the chaos of the initial outbreak, eight of the country's most dangerous murderers escaped. While being transferred across state lines to a federal holding facility, their bus overturned when they entered a town that had been overrun by the undead.

A group of five townspeople who survived soon found themselves fighting for their lives on two fronts. On one side, they had to battle to escape the advancing hordes of the undead. On the other, they had to keep a watchful eye on the gang of eight killers among them. Though these men came in handy in battling back the zombies, could they be trusted? In the end, the five survivors must choose between the undead monsters outside and the living monsters in the room.

Zombies! Eclipse of the Undead

Eclipse of the Undead takes place three days after the initial outbreak of the zombie virus. The Los Angeles coliseum was turned into a makeshift rescue station, a new temporary home to thousands of survivors ... and not all of them good people. Gang members bullied the weak and raped the defenseless. Supplies were running low, and the horde of zombies outside its gates was growing ever larger. An army unit had been protecting those inside the coliseum for days, awaiting evacuation. When word finally reached the commanding officer that the evacuation was no longer coming, he packed up his men, abandoning the coliseum and everyone in it. When the people inside realized that the soldiers were abandoning them, all hell broke loose. In the chaos, the zombies broke through the main gate and began spilling inside. Absolute bedlam ensued.

A volunteer EMT named Brad, a street-smart girl from the Barrio named Paquita, and an elderly Japanese samurai named Shigeru must fight their way clear of the coliseum. However, they must join forces with a convicted killer who has escaped custody and a homicidal gangster named Lonzo, who cares about nothing more than his precious low-rider car.

Anyone Smell That?

There is a general debate about the usefulness of a Katana against the undead. A true Japanese Katana, or *Nihonto*, would certainly be an effective tool for cleaving off (or through) the heads of zombies. However, if wielded without having first gone through the proper training in its use, some argue that you'd be more likely to just injure yourself. *Nihonto* blades are surgically sharp, and even a light touch to the edge can often cause you to cut yourself.

This part of the series depicts what may be one of the coolest zombie death scenes ever recorded. Shigeru, the Japanese sword master, realized that he had been infected. To give the others time to escape, he used himself as bait. After a moment of calm, meditative reflection, the old warrior drew his Katana and dashed headlong into a fray of zombies.

Zombies! Hunters

Zombies! Hunters takes place sometime after the chaotic days of the zombie virus outbreak. On a remote island in the Caribbean, an ex-CIA agent started a new enterprise for the thrill-seeking elite. For a substantial fee, he guided his wealthy clientele on hunts for the zombies that he allowed to wander the island. As one might imagine, it's a disaster just waiting to happen.

As the former government spook guided his latest four clients in their macabre hunt, things went south and they soon found themselves lost and surrounded by the living dead. There was no way for them to call for help. And since this little expedition of theirs was illegal, no one in the world even knew where they were. The group could rely only on their own skills to escape their predicament and return to safety—but would that be enough?

John Russo's *Escape of the Living Dead*

Escape of the Living Dead was first released by Avatar Press in October 2005. The storyline was written by John Russo, the same man who wrote the story/screenplay for *Night of the Living Dead*. This comic series is the only storyline ever to offer fans a direct sequel to the original Romero film, *Night of the Living Dead*.

Escape of the Living Dead is set in the year 1971, three years after the horrific events that took place in *Night of the Living Dead*. After a long and terrible battle, humanity was able to fight back the legions of the undead and reclaim the planet. The world of the living had only recently begun to return to a state of relative normalcy. Unfortunately, peace would be short lived.

According to a number of film and Internet sources, a movie adaptation of *Escape of the Living Dead* is currently in production. Internet buzz claims that Russo wrote the screenplay himself and that the film will star such horror legends as Tony Todd (best known for his role in *Candyman*, and who starred as Ben in the 1990 remake of *Night of the Living Dead*) and Gunnar Hansen (who played Leatherface in the original *Texas Chainsaw Massacre*). The film's release date is unknown.

In a secret military laboratory, the last remaining zombies became guinea pigs for macabre experiments. When a group of wayward outlaw bikers happened upon the facility, they saw an opportunity to make a quick score. Unfortunately, all they scored was a face full of dead people. The zombies overran the facility and eventually escaped, once again unleashing upon Earth the virus that had nearly wiped humankind from its surface.

The escaped living dead soon came upon a small rural town and began a feeding frenzy on the inhabitants. Before they moved on, the numbers of new undead swelled beyond belief. Humanity must once again find a way to destroy the living dead and contain the virus before it's too late.

Zombies: A Record of the Year of Infection (2009)

When it came to deciding how to categorize *Zombies: A Record of the Year of Infection*, it was difficult to say whether it is a piece of literature or a graphic novel. This illustrated work, written by Don Roff with art by Chris Lane, masterfully integrates elements of both mediums. Published in 2009, this zombie apocalyptic story uses elements of realism to give the reader an eerie feeling of being privy to an account of humankind's final days.

Visually speaking, the interior of *Zombies: A Record of the Year of Infection* is designed in such a way as to resemble the contents of a lost notebook. The reader learns that it is the notebook of the late Dr. Robert Twombly, an oncologist, and that it was discovered in an abandoned rural cabin in Churchill, Manitoba.

Don Roff has established himself as a prominent artist in the world of horror fiction, capable of crossing the boundaries of media and genre. Over the last decade, he has proven himself to be both a prolific horror writer and filmmaker. In 1996, he wrote, directed, and produced the short horror film *A Night in the Life of a Vampire*. His body of written work includes his debut short story collection *Scary Stories* (with creepy hand lock), published in 2006; *Creepy Stories*, another short story collection published in 2008; and *Vampire Tales*, published in 2009.

Textually, Roff makes use of the *false document technique* in order to produce a narrative that gives the illusion of authenticity. The journal is presented as Twombly's account of a period between January 5 and March 12, 2012, during which the earth is consumed by a zombie plague. As one begins reading, nothing seems out of the ordinary. The initial pages are filled with Dr. Twombly's personal journal entries and nature sketches (mainly of birds).

Moooooaaaaan...

The **false document technique** is a narrative device meant to give the reader an illusion of authenticity. This is often achieved by introducing the piece with a brief explanation of how it was discovered, indirectly claiming it to be some lost account of a real situation.

The journal's content takes a sharp turn in its entry on January 12, 2012. In this entry, Twombly explains that some mysterious virus has overtaken a nearby city, and is quickly spreading throughout the world. What follows is his record of the next three months, in which he uses his medical training in order to examine and document the conditions of those infected with the zombie virus.

War on Flesh (TokyoPop Manga)

War on Flesh is a relatively new graphic novel, released by Japanese media giant TokyoPop in fall 2009. The story is part of TokyoPop's campaign to create new *manga* using talent from outside Japan, which they dub the "Manga Revolution." The storyline was written by

Americans Justin Boring and Greg Hildebrandt. The artist of the work is also an American, Tim Smith III.

The story begins in the bayou of Louisiana, where an ancient Voodoo curse unleashed a swarm of hornets from the "Black Heart Hive." The swarm spread out from the heart of the bayou, returning the dead to unlife and transforming the living into mindless zombies. This first wave of zombies spread the curse further, ripping out the hearts of their living victims. The hearts of the slain were then replaced by hornets of the Black Heart Hive and were reanimated. The souls of those who were thusly transformed passed their energies on to the story's mysterious villain, increasing his power.

Five rebellious survivors from very conflicting backgrounds must learn to set aside their differences and work together to survive. As the harvest of souls continues, they must band together and find a way to keep the undead at bay and end the evil curse before it makes its way throughout the rest of the world.

High School of the Dead

The manga known in the United States under the title of *High School of the Dead* was originally released in Japan as *Gakuen Mokushiro* (roughly translated as "Apocalypse School/Academy"). Japanese audiences were first introduced to the manga, written by Daisuke Sato, with art by Shaito Sato, in the September 2006 edition of the *Monthly Dragon Age* magazine. The story continued its monthly run until the end of 2008, but rumors abound that Sato and Sato plan to pick it back up in the near future.

Brains!

> In spring 2008, *High School of the Dead* was translated into Spanish, this time under a less altered title of *Apocalipsis in el Instituto* (or "Apocalypse in the Institute"). Though mainly distributed in Spain, copies of the Spanish version are finding their way to other Spanish-speaking countries, and the story is growing in popularity among Mexican manga fans.

The story of *High School of the Dead* is set at Fujimi High School during the outbreak of a zombie apocalypse. The initial outbreak killed nearly everyone on campus, transforming them into flesh-eating zombies. A handful of students and the school's resident nurse are the only survivors, and they must team up to survive.

While the story has multiple characters, it focuses primarily on 17-year-old sophomore Takashi Komuro and his female childhood friend, Rei. Takashi has been in love with Rei his entire life. When they were little, Rei once promised that she would marry him when they grew up. As a little boy, however, Takashi did not know how to react to Rei's feelings and thought she was just joking around. Over the years, his difficulty in interacting with Rei and accepting the fact that she also loves him caused ripples in their friendship.

Despite Takashi's own doubts about his abilities, his consistently solid decisions and repeated demonstrations of his willingness to protect everyone, even at the risk of his life, led the members of the group to follow and respect him. His feelings for Rei often gave Takashi courage to act in the face of grave danger, sometimes even when he perhaps shouldn't.

Aside from Takashi and Rei, the group consisted of several other colorful characters:

- **Saeko Busujima:** President of the girls' Kendo (swordplay) club and a senior. Her ability to effectively kill zombies with a *bokken* (wooden sword) made her a valuable asset to the group. Despite her superior fighting skills, she wholeheartedly believed in Takashi's leadership. She also struggled to reconcile her feelings about the thrill she received from zombie killing.

- **Kota Hirano:** This sophomore may have been the target of the school bullies, but he was an expert on guns, the only one in the group. His skills with firearms made him valuable to the group. He escaped the school with Saya, though only because he followed her directions (up to that point, he had been panicking).

- **Shizuka Marikawa:** The very busty, rather air-headed 26-year-old school nurse. She lived with a sniper on the urban Japanese Special Assault Team and allowed the group to use her home as shelter after their escape from the school.

◆ **Saya Takagi:** Sixteen-year-old daughter of a political family (though she isn't too fond of her parents) and very intelligent (she calls herself a "genius"), she became a strategist of sorts for the group. She escaped from the school with the help of Kota and, like Rei, was a childhood friend of Takashi.

The Least You Need to Know

◆ *Marvel Zombies* takes places in an alternate universe where the world's superheroes have been infected with a zombie virus.

◆ The *Deadworld* series is unique, in that it depicts a ruling class of zombies that are intelligent and organized.

◆ Russo's *Escape of the Living Dead* is the only storyline that offers a legitimate direct sequel to *Night of the Living Dead*.

◆ *War on Flesh* falls back on the old Voodoo zombie by offering an updated view of the so-called "Voodoo zombie curse."

◆ *High School of the Dead* is the most popular zombie-based manga storyline currently available.

Chapter 8

Zombie Comics on the Web

In This Chapter

- The world of web comics
- The zombie and human hierarchies of *The Zombie Hunters*
- The gritty zombie apocalypse, *Last Blood*
- The surreal world of the undead as depicted in *Everyday Decay*
- *Slaughter, Inc.*, and its commentary on capitalism in a zombie-apocalyptic world

The rise of the Internet has opened up a number of new avenues by which aspiring writers and artists can make their voices heard and their work seen. For those looking to make their way into the world of comic books, web comics offer a convenient springboard. In recent years, a number of popular titles have emerged that have zombies at their cores. From serious to comical, to a little bit of both, zombie-themed web comics have taken the Net by storm. A simple web search yields enough results to fill up a book. This chapter offers but a sampling of the zombie web comic titles available.

The Zombie Hunters

You can find Jenny Romanchuk's web comic, *The Zombie Hunters*, at www.thezombiehunters.com. Her stories depict a very different world, in which humans have had to develop ways to live with the zombie infection. The last human civilizations were broken up into specific groups, and whether one was infected had a heavy impact on how one was treated.

Brains!

Probably one of the most flexible aspects of any zombie story is the nature/behavior of the zombie virus. Since it's a purely hypothetical virus, it often leaves writers with some room for creative flexibility. And each zombie story often has its own unique spin on how this particular zombie virus works.

Segregation in a Post-Zombie World

In Romanchuk's world, the zombie virus itself was not fatal. If a person became infected while still alive, the virus remained dormant until he or she died. Because of this, the inhabitants of the Argus Research Center (A.R.C.), the last human refuge, were separated into specific groups:

- **Uninfected civilians:** Simply put, these individuals had survived the outbreak without being infected. They were guarded and their needs were well cared for as long as they followed the rules of the compound. The children at the facility, regardless of their infection status, were always cared for and properly educated.

- **Infected civilians:** Although they were not mistreated, they were kept in a fenced quarantine area separating them from the uninfected members of the population. Any sense of freedom beyond the quarantine zone often required them to do a certain amount of dirty work, as you will see.

- **Red Halo Officers:** These were the enforcers of the A.R.C. facility. Red Halo was a well-trained and heavily armed military force, consisting primarily of former armed forces members. In the A.R.C., the Red Halo was the law. Despite the fact that they were supposed to protect the populace, the officers were regarded with a certain amount of fear.

- **Facility staff:** This group consisted of quarantine staff, doctors, scientists, researchers, and so on. For the most part, they worked tirelessly to understand and hopefully find a way to cure the zombie virus.

- **Zombie hunters:** This group was the backbone of the A.R.C., though one would never guess it by the way they were treated. They were recruited from infected civilians in the quarantine zone and were sent on salvage/raid missions in areas outside the compound, so as not to risk exposing the uninfected. The job was horrific and stressful, and most of the veteran members were a little "left of center," since any totally sane person usually broke under the pressure after only one or two missions.

All Zombies Are Not Created Equal

In Romanchuk's post-apocalyptic world, not all zombies were created equal. A number of unique types of undead existed, each with their own special strengths, weaknesses, and weird quirks. The zombies that her hunters had to face on a regular basis included the following types:

- **Basilisks:** These were believed to be the most intelligent zombie type. For example, they were known to pretend to be a dead body until a victim drew near enough to look them in the eyes. Their eyes were their main weapon, producing a strange glow that paralyzed victims. Prolonged eye contact led to a painful seizure that ended in complete loss of muscle control (the victim went limp). Then the zombie ate the victim.

- **Berserkers:** These zombies were rare, and that's probably a good thing. They were not only very smart, but also horribly sadistic. These zombies used stabbing weapons to prolong the agony of their victims, which they seemed to enjoy. A Berserker zombie did not start feeding until it had tortured its victims to the point that they no longer responded to pain. Then it ate them.

- **Crawlers:** These were the typical zombies—slow, weak, clumsy, and stupid. However, in large numbers, they presented a formidable threat. Another problem was that other, more lethal zombie types sometimes masked their presence by hiding among a mob of Crawlers until they saw an opportunity to strike.

- **Howlers:** These zombies were just as weak and slow as Crawlers, and from 10 or more meters away they weren't much of a threat. Less than that, however, and they could cripple their victims with an ear-piercing wail that caused nausea, dizziness, and unconsciousness.

- **Hunters:** Another relatively intelligent, or at least very patient, zombie type. They were skilled trackers/stalkers, and often their victims didn't even know they were being targeted until it was too late. They were the most agile type and had been known to track targets for months without losing interest.

- **Mercy zombies:** These were the most unique zombie type, and no other depiction like this has ever been created. These zombies used a somewhat merciful method for killing their victims. They hugged their victims and bit a major artery. They then gently held and rocked the victim, even making calming cooing sounds until the person drifted off to death. Some uninfected people even sought out mercy zombies as a form of suicide, viewing them as angels of death and mercy.

- **Spitters:** This zombie type was considered the most deadly. This was the only class that could kill from a long distance, by spitting a highly corrosive acid (sometimes as far as a football field's length).

To read about the adventures of Jenny Romanchuk's eccentric team of *Zombie Hunters*, visit her website at www.thezombiehunters.com, where you can view episodes for free.

Last Blood

Last Blood, a collaborative web comic by Bobby and Chris Crosby, put a unique spin on the zombie apocalypse. In a small U.S. town, a band of about 30 survivors struggled to stay alive. But the waves of undead were getting larger as time went on. One day, just as it seemed they were about to be overrun, a pair of incredibly skilled, fast, and strong individuals came to their aid. When the smoke cleared, they introduced themselves as Matheson and Valerie. And they explained that they were vampires and had come for their blood (prompting the town school-teacher to shoot Matheson in the chest ... which, of course, did nothing).

Braial!

Many consider the old "vampires vs. zombies" concept to be a cliché joke. However, Crosby's story avoids the usual mistake of focusing on the conflict and instead follows a character focused storyline that makes the concept interesting—probably for the first time.

Vampires rely on the blood of living human beings to survive. The problem here was that the hordes of zombies had quickly turned live humans into a rare commodity. Blood was in short supply. As a result, the vampires were on a mission to gather together and protect the last remaining humans on the planet. Groups were sent to human strongholds all over the world. Unfortunately, the only survivors they had found were these rural Americans.

It turned out that the vampires were, in a way, responsible for the zombie outbreak. If a vampire went for too long without blood, he or she didn't die. Instead, the vampire turned into a Schemiacs, a dead, rotting corpse on a feeding binge—something like a zombie. The original Schemiac responsible for the outbreak had the power to telepathically control the zombie hordes, and he soon brought thousands of walking dead to the survivors' doorstep. Soon a battle royale pitted 500 vampires and less than 30 human survivors against thousands upon thousands of zombies.

Everyday Decay

Since the zombie apocalypse, things had returned somewhat to normal for Dorian and his wife, Emiko ("Emi," for short) ... aside from the pesky zombies they had to deal with when they went out for a night on the town. As the only living survivors in town, they pretty much had the run of the place. They had killed most of the undead over the many months since the outbreak, so they only had to keep an eye out for the occasional straggler. They had no jobs to worry about. No laws to worry about. No mortgage to pay. The worst problem Dorian had to deal with on a daily basis was his wife's often troublesome and always ill-behaved dog, TyTy—a very tiny, *very* fluffy French Papillon. All in all, however, they had a pretty sweet little setup, especially considering that it was the end of the world and all.

Brains!

In looking at most zombie films, it might seem that we humans fear one another more than we fear zombies. In a significant number of zombie stories, the protagonists meet their demise not at the hands and teeth of the undead: they usually die at the hands of the living.

Dorian liked things the way they were and preferred to frighten off any visitors who happened through town than risk the relative peace and safety he and his wife had. The problem is, not all visitors were so willing to be scared off. When they saw what appeared to be a person under attack by zombies, Emi convinced (okay, forced) Dorian to help her intervene. The whole thing turned out to be an ambush. The two were taken captive and learned that their captors intended to use them as guinea pigs for a vaccine they were trying to develop for the zombie virus, which they were deriving from the blood of a member of their group whom they believed to be immune. There was only one problem ... he wasn't immune. The guy, Mathias, had fabricated bite wounds to convince them of his immunity so they would have a reason to keep him alive. Dorian and Emi then had to battle their way clear of the madman's circus they suddenly found themselves involved in. Would this be the end of their happy days of post-apocalyptic marital bliss? And who would feed the dog?

Slaughter, Inc.

Slaughter, Inc., written by Tom Oliver-Martin, with art by Kuba Kujawa, followed the exploits of arms dealer Gregory Heathcliff. He made his living selling weapons to militias, gangs, and terrorist groups. As the world went insane, however, and was overrun by hordes of flesh-hungry zombies, Gregory smelled opportunity. Making his fortune out of the world's ruin, he used the zombie apocalypse to sell his wares of mass destruction to the highest bidders.

When the infrastructures of the world collapsed under the weight of the zombie invasion, Gregory took his company *Slaughter, Inc.*, global. He decided that war profiteering was small change compared to the money he could make arming the general public. He headed from town to dell. Weapons were his business ... and business was booming.

The Least You Need to Know

- *The Zombie Hunters* is a well-developed web comic that has special hierarchies for both its human protagonists and zombie nemeses.

- *Last Blood* is probably the most successful "zombie vs. vampires" story.

- *Everyday Decay* tells the story of a young married couple living happily in the wake of a zombie apocalypse ... until other humans showed up and made a mess of it all.

- *Slaughter, Inc.*, shows how the world's misfortune is one man's golden ticket, following an amoral arms dealer who used the zombie apocalypse to make a killing (pun intended).

Part 3

Zombie Cinema and Pop Culture

Where would zombies be without the medium of cinema? In fact, few could argue with the fact that the modern zombie concept was born on the silver screen. In Part 3, we take a look at how the genre of zombie cinema has evolved over the last half-century—from the groundbreaking works of legendary zombie-film director George A. Romero to the many who followed in his example. We look at the many films that make up the "zombie canon" of undead films. In contrast, we also discuss the rotten side of the zombie film coin by looking at some of the worst zombie films ever made.

Chapter 9

Early Zombie Films

In This Chapter

- ◆ The Voodoo-based nature of early zombie cinema
- ◆ *White Zombie*, the first horror film to feature zombies
- ◆ The pseudo-sequel and second zombie film, *Revolt of the Zombies*
- ◆ *Ouanga*, the little-known film that some say is the true "second zombie film ever made"
- ◆ The World War II–era zombie comedy *King of the Zombies*
- ◆ The 1943 zombie film *I Walked with a Zombie*

Zombies first entered the world of moving pictures in the twentieth century and have only grown in popularity since. These first zombie films, however, were often associated with the Voodoo-style zombie (see Chapter 1) and not the viral zombies that are portrayed in cinema today. Many of these early zombie films were set in the Caribbean Islands in order to give them a more "authentic" feel (though a number of these movies used an island that doesn't exist). Some of these early zombie movies even brought the walking dead into the realm of comedy for the very first time.

White Zombie (1932)

The 1932 film *White Zombie* is all about "firsts." First of all (ha ha), it was the very first zombie film ever made. United Artists released it to the American public in August 1932. At the time, "moving pictures," as movies were then called, had only recently included sound. As a result, *White Zombie* was more than just the first zombie movie; it was also the first horror movie that was not a silent film. However, this has not affected its cult status as the original film of the zombie cinema genre, mainly because it was also the first independent horror film to star Bela Lugosi, most well known for his previous role in the 1931 *Dracula* film (as Count Dracula). Today, Lugosi is considered an iconic figure of early horror cinema. He went on to make a number of these kinds of independent films, despite the fact that doing so seems to have somewhat damaged his status as a "serious actor" in the eyes of the Hollywood elite.

Brains!

You have probably heard "White Zombie" before, just not in *this* context. Most people know it as the name of the heavy metal group fronted by lead vocalist, writer, director, and avid horror cinema enthusiast Rob Zombie. If you have ever wondered where they got the band's name, now you know: it was inspired by the 1932 film that spawned the zombie and horror film genres.

The screenplay for *White Zombie* was written by Garnett Weston, and the film was directed by Victor Halperin. However, Halperin ran into serious money troubles and eventually quit the project well before the movie was completed (though his brother Edward managed to keep the name Halperin Productions in the film). Actor Bela Lugosi was allowed to take over the direction of the remainder of the film. This is impressive, considering that he also played a major role in the film as a villainous and mysterious white man named Murder who stole the secrets of Voodoo in order to create his own army of zombie slaves to work his plantation and carry out his every whim.

Brains!

Hollywood actors were not always as well paid as they are today. Bela Lugosi was paid only $800 (even in 1932, that wasn't much money) for his performance in *White Zombie,* and he was the highest-paid actor in the movie. He is known to have expressed regret about this. He felt that the Halperin brothers and the film's distributors made far more than most independent filmmakers of the time. *White Zombie* grossed less than $25,000 at the box office. Considering that the film's budget was an estimated $50,000, this would seem to be a misperception by Lugosi.

The film began with a young couple boarding a carriage at night, shortly after their arrival in Haiti. They are Neil Parker (played by John Harron) and his fiancée, Madeleine Short (played by Madge Bellamy). As the two lovebirds rode along in the carriage driven by their hired Haitian driver, their journey was interrupted when they came upon a group of people chanting as they buried a dead body in the dirt road. When Neil asked the driver what was happening, he explained that these people were burying the body in the road so that it would not be stolen from its grave. Since people regularly frequented the road, he told Neil, the body wouldn't be an easy target for grave robbers. After this, the driver lashed the horses forward and the carriage rocked as they drove right over the fresh burial (or the dead body—it's hard to tell on screen and the film never specifies this detail).

Don't Get Bit!

It may not be an intentional element of zombie films, but they often address and break down racial stereotypes of the time (many perpetuated by the cinematic industry). The Haitian carriage driver (musician Clarence Muse) didn't perform in line with stereotypical portrayals of blacks in 1930s films. Blacks were often depicted as easily panicked, mentally slow, and subservient to whites. However, Muse appeared calm, intelligent, and assertive in his scene. When Harron's character chastised him for driving so fast to escape, saying, "We might've been killed!" Muse didn't give the stereotypical "Yessuh" response associated with many black characters of the time. He replied, "Worse than that, Monsieur. We might have been caught." An assertive black character would also be part of the next landmark zombie film, *Night of the Living Dead* (see Chapter 10).

As they moved on slowly, a strange man approached the carriage with his sinister eyes fixed intently upon Madeleine. He placed his hand on her scarf, which was draped over the edge of the carriage window. The driver saw him and then looked to the hillside by the road and saw a group of blank-faced men stumbling toward them. "Zombies!" he cried out, and whipped the horses to a full gallop. As they sped away, Madeleine's scarf was ripped from her neck. Holding it in his hands, the man watched them drive away. This mysterious stranger was a man named Murder Legendre (though in the film he is referred to by name only once, and even then simply as "Murder").

Having survived their frightening encounter, the two arrived safely at their destination, the luxurious home of a wealthy gentleman named Charles Beaumont, played by Robert Frazer (who, coincidentally, was the first actor to play Robin Hood on the silver screen). They recently met Beaumont while in the nearby city of Port-au-Prince, and when he learned of their plans to marry, he insisted on paying for their wedding and hosting it at his mansion. While there, they also met a local, pipe-smoking Christian missionary by the name of Dr. Bruner (played by Joseph Cawthorn), who was scheduled to conduct their wedding ceremony. Bruner, however, expressed his feelings of distrust for Beaumont and urged Neil and Madeleine to leave Haiti as soon as they were married, and to cease their dealings with him.

Bruner's instincts about Beaumont were dead on. The rich Beaumont did not do this out of the goodness of his heart. He was infatuated with Madeleine and brought them to his mansion to find some way by which to seduce her and take her from Neil. Seeing how in love they were, however, Beaumont enlisted the help of Murder Legendre. He had heard of Legendre's powers, including his ability to create zombies, and convinced him to use his powers to make Madeleine love him. Love, however, doesn't work this way. Murder told Beaumont that the only way Madeleine would be his would be to make her a zombie. At first, Beaumont was repulsed by the suggestion. But he took the zombie potion from Murder nonetheless. And on the night of her marriage to Neil, Beaumont slipped the potion to Madeleine. She "died" and was immediately buried.

Neil, as one would expect, was overcome with grief. So he did what many men would do in such a situation—he got falling-down drunk on rum. In his inebriated state, however, he had a vision of Madeleine that convinced him she was still alive. And, in fact, she sort of was ... Murder and Beaumont had already resurrected her as a mindless zombie. Barely able to walk due to intoxication, Neil managed to find Dr. Bruner to tell him about his vision. Bruner suspected that Madeleine had been turned into a zombie and took Neil (still *very* drunk) to see a local "witch doctor" who was quite familiar with Murder—he was the only man ever taken into Murder's castle fortress who returned alive and "unzombified." It would seem that Murder was able to force the witch doctor to divulge the secrets of his magic before he managed to escape. Not wanting to tempt fate, the witch doctor refused to help them.

So Neil and Dr. Bruner ventured on toward Murder's castle fortress. This became complicated by the level of Neil's drunkenness, and they had to stop to let him lie down. As Bruner wandered away, Neil again had a vision of Madeleine. This time, he saw her standing at the balcony of Murder's castle. He stumbled off by himself, intent on saving his beloved, no matter how intoxicated he was.

Back at the castle, Beaumont began to feel remorse about what he had done to Madeleine. He begged Murder to reverse it, but Murder refused. In his shame, Beaumont devoured a bottle of wine. Unfortunately for him, Murder laced it with zombie potion. Beaumont learned too late that he had been betrayed. Murder wanted Madeleine for himself, and he stood coldly by as he watched Beaumont's calm yet agonizing zombie transformation.

About this time, Neil managed to sneak into the castle (stumbling, falling, and swaying the entire time). Murder seemed to sense Neil's presence as he collapsed on a divan at the top of a nearby staircase—or he just heard him stumbling around the castle drunk (it's hard to tell). Yes, that's right, our heroic Neil passed out drunk on the hallway furniture of his sworn enemy. While he was snoozing, Murder clasped his hands together (apparently, this is how his magic works?) and summoned Madeleine from her bed. He handed her a carving knife and ordered her to kill her passed-out husband. She raised the knife but hesitated for a moment, as if she was remembering who she was—and who she was about to stab to death. A shot of Lugosi's eyes suggested that he was struggling to strengthen his hold on her zombified mind. Either that or he was constipated. (A lot of things are hard to follow in this film, but it is still a classic.) Then something inexplicable happened.

Brains!

> The Halperin brothers originally planned for *White Zombie* to be a screen adaptation of a recent play by Kenneth S. Webb, which they had seen in February of that year, entitled *Zombie*. In the end, however, they went with a *slightly* different story. However, this did not stop Webb from suing them for stealing his idea. The only problem was that the stories weren't identical enough to prove infringement, so the only thing that could be pointed to was the fact that both works had "Zombie" in their titles. Needless to say, the court ruled that *zombie* was a general term and could not, therefore, be owned by anyone. The Halperin brothers won and Webb had to abandon his suit.

Beaumont was still struggling to resist the effects of the zombie potion. The camera cut from Madeleine holding the knife, to Murder, back to Madeleine, to Beaumont at the table, back to Madeleine, to what appeared to be a close-up shot of the side of Beaumont's neck (as already said, some things are hard to follow in this movie). She raised the knife again and, just as she was about to bring it plunging down, a hand reached out from behind the large black curtains beside her, taking hold of her wrist and stopping her from killing Neil. Some say this is supposed to be Beaumont's hand … but how can it be his hand if he is at the table at the bottom of the stairs? Also, as soon as her wrist was grabbed, Madeleine dropped the knife and just sort of wandered away. She dashed out onto the castle's cliff-side balcony just as Neil came to, holding his head as if it was about to pop. He called out to her and took off in pursuit when she did not respond. He found her wobbling back and forth at the edge of the precarious ocean-side cliff on which the castle sat. He pulled her to safety and unsuccessfully tried to snap her out of her trance.

Brains!

> Though the movie never clarifies this point, some have speculated that the mysterious hand that emerges from behind the curtain is actually that of Dr. Bruner. In truth, he does appear on the balcony shortly after this, which at least suggests that he was in the castle around that time.

Murder emerged from the castle and again clasped his hands together. His mob of zombies descended upon Neil, and they began pushing him toward the cliff. He drew a revolver from his pocket (apparently, he was saving it?) and opened fire. He hit one zombie square in the chest, but it just kept on coming. In the nick of time, Dr. Bruner snuck up behind Murder and knocked him out with what appears to be a leather sap (which, admittedly, would be a rather odd object for a missionary to be carrying around ... but anyway). Neil jumped aside, and the zombies just kept waddling forward as if on autopilot. They seemed to be continuing the last action they were commanded to perform before their master was knocked out cold. The lot of them went toppling off the cliff. Even Beaumont's recently zombified butler, trusty old Silver (played by Brandon Hurst), went over the edge.

Murder came around and snuck back to the castle stairs. He again clasped his hands together. But before he could pull any more "bad juju," Beaumont used his last shred of free will to shove Murder over the cliff. Unfortunately, turning into a zombie is "murder" (get it?) on one's coordination. Beaumont toppled forward and joined Murder as a big red greasy spot on the rocks below.

Brains!

> *White Zombie* is public domain, meaning that no one owns the rights to the film anymore. This also means that it can be legally shown, copied, reproduced, and distributed by just about anyone. So don't bother buying it on DVD. Tons of Internet film archives have the movie in its entirety. You can even find the whole film on multiple YouTube channels. If you do decide to watch the film, pay close attention to the zombie butler, Silver (Brandon Hurst), as he goes over the edge. The falling zombie-actors were actually jumping into a pool of water. Apparently, Hurst decided that he should hold his nose just before he went over. So look for the zombie who holds his nose closed, as if about to go swimming, just before he falls over.

Once Murder died, Madeleine was freed from his control. She slowly transformed back into her old, bubbly self. In her final return to normalcy, she looked Neil in the eyes and delivered the cheese-ridden line, "I ... I dreamed." Neil, likely figuring that a slightly brain-damaged wife was better than nothing, simply embraced her without much reply.

As he went to kiss her, Dr. Bruner tapped him roughly on the shoulder. He stood there with his ivory pipe and asked if anyone had a match. Umm … the end. No, seriously. That was how they ended it.

Revolt of the Zombies (1936)

Revolt of the Zombies, simply put, was an attempt by the Halperin brothers to cash in on the semi-success of *White Zombie,* which, by this time, they had lost the rights to due to their inability to pay back the many debts they had accumulated for its production. While *White Zombie* is seen as a somewhat cheesy but still enjoyable classic, *Revolt of the Zombies* is not. First of all, the zombies (which were still supposedly created by magical or supernatural means) were no longer in Haiti. Nope, for this film, the Halperin brothers, for their own unknown reasons, decided to make Buddhist monks in Cambodia the source of this film's zombies. Anyone who is even slightly familiar with Buddhism can tell you why there are many things wrong with this. Namely, they believe in the law of karma (basically, "What goes around, comes around"), and desecrating the bodies of the dead for one's own personal gain would *definitely* build up a lot of bad karma. And anyone who is even slightly familiar with Voodoo can tell you that there probably weren't a whole lot of adherents living in French Cambodia during World War I. And if there were, they wouldn't likely be Buddhist monks.

A French military unit stationed on the Franco-Austrian border (and, by the way, every soldier in the "French" unit has an American accent) learned through eyewitness accounts that a local Cambodian Buddhist priest was creating hordes of unstoppable zombie soldiers to protect his village from German invaders. So they brought in the priest for inter-rogation, and the commanding officer, Colonel Mazovia (played by Roy D'Arcy), demanded that he create a regiment of zombie soldiers for them as well. The monk refused to do this and, for his defiance, was sentenced (right then and there, without any sort of a trial) to life in a military prison.

While in the brig awaiting transfer, the monk removed a hidden piece of parchment from his robes and prepared to burn it. This parchment contained a map to the location of the secret formula and incantations needed for creating zombies. Before he was able to destroy it, however,

Colonel Mazovia murdered the monk and took the parchment (which was partially burned) off the dead body.

Fast-forward to the days immediately after the close of World War I. The Allies sent an expedition to Cambodia. Their mission was to recover (or, if they couldn't, destroy) the secret to creating zombies. Colonel Mazovia led the expedition, which consisted of General Duval (George Cleveland), his daughter Claire (Dorothey Stone), a linguistics expert named Armand Louque (played by Dead Jagger), and an English chap named Clifford Grayson (played by Robert Nolan).

A weird love triangle was going on among Claire, Armand, and Clifford. Apparently, Armand loved Claire. But Claire loved Clifford. And Clifford was completely clueless that Claire had recently accepted Armand's proposal of marriage only to make him jealous. In all honesty, most of the movie is about the drama related to what's going down among these three characters. Very little of it actually deals with zombies.

Armand later broke off his engagement to Claire because he saw her rush into Clifford's arms when a support rope snapped and brought a tree swing crashing to the ground. Seeing this, Armand realized that Claire truly loved Clifford. Armand felt betrayed, knowing that his beloved fiancée agreed to marry him when her heart belonged to another man.

Soon after all this drama, Armand went off alone and stumbled upon some sort of monastic ritual. He followed a local monk to a secluded temple, where he discovered the secret location of the zombie parchment. Instead of destroying it, or bringing it to the others, he decided to keep the power for himself. He created his own zombies, with the intention of taking revenge on Clifford by turning Claire into a zombie. After this point, the movie is just a revised, relocated version of the second half of *White Zombie*. Just like its predecessor, *Revolt of the Zombies* is public domain, so you can find it all over the Internet on sites such as YouTube; IMBD.com also has archive links to the film.

Ouanga (1936)

Released in the same year as *Revolt of the Zombies*, *Ouanga* is by some considered the rightful heir to the title of "second zombie film ever made." In fact, there are many who speculate (and with good reason) that the racial politics during the first half of the twentieth century likely played a role in this. Also known by the alternate titles *Love Wanga* and *Drums of the Jungle,* this film was ahead of its time in many ways. Whether or not it was the second film ever to feature zombies, it was undeniably one of the very first films to depict romantic situations that involved an interracial couple.

Brains!

Ouanga may be set in Haiti, but it was not filmed there. The film was originally supposed to be filmed on location in Haiti. However, this had to be changed early on. Shortly after the movie's crew arrived to set up in Haiti, the locals got wind of what the movie was about—namely, that it was about Voodoo. This caused such a terrible uproar that the film's production had to be halted and a new location secured in Jamaica.

Adam (played by Philip Brandon) was the son of a white plantation owner in Haiti, and he came to the island for two years in order to work his father's lands. Soon after his arrival, Adam caught the eye of Clelie (played by Fredi Washington), the wealthy, young, and powerful Haitian woman who owned the neighboring plantation. She came on to him, and Adam returned her affections. The two carried on a love affair for two years. When Adam decided it was time to stop fooling around and wanted to get serious and settle down, he cast Clelie aside. She repeatedly begged him not to leave her, even humiliating herself by groveling on her knees ... but all for naught. Adam had his white fiancée Eve (played by Marie Paxton) shipped to the island so that they could be married.

Brains!

You may have noticed that the name of Adam's fiancée is Eve. That's right ... this would make them Adam and Eve. Try not to read into that too much. It will give you a headache.

Adam failed to realize two things: First, Shakespeare was right that "Hell hath no fury like a woman scorned"; and second, Clelie was also a Voodoo priestess. When she finally realized that Adam had permanently cast her aside like garbage so that he could marry his white fiancée, Clelie's heartache turned to rage. In fact, she said, "I'm trash to him. Good for nothing trash. Black trash."

Brains!

A remake of *Ouanga* was released in 1939, under the title *The Devil's Daughter*. This new version of the film, which had an all-black cast, completely removed all traces of interracial love affairs. This movie was both set and shot in Jamaica. The conflict in this film revolves around a land dispute between two sisters over the distribution of their late father's plantation. Voodoo and zombies are still present, though this film is seen by many as a poor attempt at remaking what was a revolutionary (if somewhat ill-received and mistakenly intended) film.

Clelie used a Voodoo charm called *Ouanga* to create a pair of zombie minions to kidnap Eve so that she could be sacrificed in ritual. Strong and enraged, Clelie loudly proclaimed, "I'll show him what a black woman can do!" And she certainly did. The obscurity of this film makes it difficult to find. It was shunned in many countries, and among both blacks and whites. Many whites (and blacks) did not like the fact that it portrayed an interracial affair, despite the fact that the film's "moral" was basically that such affairs are dangerous and should be avoided. Today, many people shun the movie *because* of its anti-interracial message.

King of the Zombies (1941)

King of the Zombies is not nearly as serious and frightening as its title suggests. In fact, it is more of a comedy than a horror film. Written by Edmond Kelso and directed by Jean Yarbrough, this is probably one of the most misrepresented zombie films of all time. It was marketed with movie posters that offered such spooky taglines as:

> HUMAN SACRIFICES! SAVAGE TORTURE! VOODOO RITES!

And:

> "Blood-chilling revelations of the weird cult that practices its black magic in the impenetrable jungles of Central America!" (Which is a particularly odd tagline, considering that the film takes place nowhere near Central America, but on a small Caribbean island somewhere between Cuba and Puerto Rico.)

And perhaps the most misleading of all:

> If you can sit through this spine-tingling carnival of shrieks and howls without getting the thrill of a lifetime ... you must belong to the living dead.

This movie is actually one of many comedic films starring black comedian actor Mantan Moreland, whose prolific body of cinematic works is as controversial as it is legendary. This movie stands out among all other zombie films for this reason. You see, Moreland's comedy is seen by many as a perpetuation of the racial stereotypes about blacks that were prevalent in the 1930s, '40s, and '50s. Moreland, though often very funny, is viewed today as an example of the attitudes that led to negative misperceptions about African Americans. This is quite contrary to the usual rebellious elements of zombie films, which commonly use zombies to illustrate the wrongs of a society. Mantan Moreland's *King of the Zombies* character, for example, is a black butler named Jefferson Jackson, is easily frightened, prone to panic, uneducated, wildly superstitious, and not very well spoken. Because of this, opinions about his works tend to vary from one person to another. On the one hand, he was involved in producing many of the very first all-black-cast films ever made. On the other hand, his characters often played to racial stereotypes.

The movie takes place during World War II (at the time, however, America was not yet involved in it). A small plane, piloted by James "Mac" McCarthy (played by Dick Purcell), was low on fuel and lost in a violent storm somewhere over the Caribbean between Cuba and Puerto Rico on its way to the Bahamas. Another pilot had recently gone missing in the same area, and his whereabouts were unknown. Mac was accompanied by his friend Bill Summers (played by John Archer) and his butler, Jefferson (Moreland). Flying on fumes, Mac picked up a sudden radio transmission, though in a language he did not understand. He knew that such a strong transmission meant a transmitter was in the immediate area. He took the plane down and made a rather ungraceful crash landing on a small island.

The three men regrouped and soon found a house on the island. They met the owner, the mysterious Dr. Mikhlos Sangre (or Mikhail ... available film credits vary on his first name, likely because he says it with a very thick accent that is hard to follow), played by Henry Victor (though the role was originally meant for Bela Lugosi, who turned it down). Sangre lived there with his wife and servants, but he said little else about why he was there. He told them that he did not have a radio on the island, which Mac found suspicious, since a transmitter had to send out the signal he had received on the plane. Exhausted from their ordeal, however, Mac and Bill were shown to the house's guest rooms and Jefferson joined Sangre's servants in the kitchen.

The servants spooked Jefferson and told him that he must sleep in the kitchen, warning him to pay no attention to anything he saw and heard after midnight. He tried to sleep, but shortly after the clock struck midnight, he was shocked awake by a pair of zombies lumbering toward him. He rushed out in a panic and went to find Mac and Bill. They allowed him to sleep in their room for the night, but Jefferson was again given a fright when he saw a woman in white come out of a secret door in the wall and head toward Mac. She stopped short, however, and scurried off just as Jefferson woke the other two men. They decided to investigate, hoping that maybe their search would lead them to a transmitter. They found something far more bizarre.

In the basement, they stumbled upon Dr. Sangre and several of his servants in the process of performing a "zombie ritual" on a man strapped to a chair. This man was Admiral Arthur Wainwright, the aviator who recently had gone missing in the area. Sangre planned to use the zombie ritual to force Wainwright to divulge military intelligence secrets. It turned out that Sangre was actually a spy "for a European government," although they never specifically say *which* European government. Sangre claimed to be Austrian, but he spoke German to his family and in his radio transmission. Why would they leave such a detail unspoken? Well, keep in mind that the United States was not yet involved in World War II, and didn't want to be. The country had only recently been involved in one "Great War," and it had no intention of getting into another. So it wouldn't have been prudent for an American film to directly say that the villain, even of a comedy, was a "Nazi spy."

Jefferson thought he was a zombie for a little while, but one of Sangre's (rather attractive) female servants convinced him that he was not. Mac was not so lucky and became zombified (or, at least, it seems that is what happened). Bill finally confronted Sangre in the middle of his occult rite. At this point in the ritual, something went awry. It is hard to say exactly what went wrong because the film doesn't make much sense from this point. Regardless, for some unknown reason all the zombies in the room suddenly turned on their master, Dr. Sangre. In one of the final scenes of the film, Bill thanked Jefferson for getting the zombies to turn on Sangre. So perhaps there is some overly subtle detail meant to tell us that Jefferson was responsible for this (or perhaps there is not).

The "zombie" Mac at first joined Sangre's other zombies as they approached Bill, ordered by their master to attack. However, Mac stopped when Bill called out to him, and suddenly turned toward Sangre (still acting like a zombie). The other zombies followed his lead, and all of them turned on their master. Sangre's Voodoo servants screamed in terror and fled. He continued to order them to stop, trying to regain control of the situation. He pulled out a revolver and started busting some caps into the zombies, but they kept on coming. He even shot Mac several times at point-blank range, but he didn't even slow down (though we also don't see any bullet wounds). During the chaos, Bill freed Sangre's captives. Mac eventually backed Sangre to a large open-fire hearth, and the creepy doctor fell back into the flames to his doom.

With Sangre dead, Mac was unzombified and even survived (despite being shot in the chest multiple times at point-blank range). Bill told Admiral Wainwright, who had just called in the Coast Guard from Sangre's radio transmitter, that Mac would "just need a little patching up." Ah, the miracles of modern medicine.

I Walked with a Zombie (1943)

Many of the movies already discussed in this chapter involve sensational, sometimes purely imaginary elements of Voodoo. *I Walked with a Zombie* stands apart in this regard. In all truth, the film offers a far more accurate portrayal of Haitian Voodoo. There are no hand-clasping men with waxed eyebrows, as in *White Zombie*. There are no ridiculous geographic relocations, as in *Revolt of the Zombies*. In fact, for a movie that was made in 1943, *I Walked with a Zombie* was rather progressive in its fairly rational and relatively fair treatment of the Voodoo religion. For example, none of the main characters referred to Vodun *houngans/mambos* as "witch doctors." They used the proper terms for Haitian elements, such as calling the Vodun abode a *humfort*, instead of referring to it as a "Voodoo Temple" or some other anglicized misnomer.

I Walked with a Zombie was written and produced by Val Lewton. Lewton was quickly gaining a solid reputation for himself in the film industry as a man who could be handed nothing more than a movie title and, with his team of writers, create a solid plotline and working script out of it. Lewton could do this because he had a knack for surrounding himself with talented, hardworking people, and this attribute made him a very effective movie producer. He rewarded creativity and hard work, and he had no time or patience for people who didn't pull their own weight. To ensure that *I Walked with a Zombie* had the spooky, surreal, yet believable feel needed to match his storyline, Lewton turned to the more experienced noir-style film director Jacques Tourneur (best known for his noir cinema classic *Cat People*). Of course, Tourneur was also a headstrong man. He despised anything that he felt put limits on him, such as being told what the title of his movie was going to be. Regardless, the two men worked well together in this film, and Lewton would draw on this experience to create a later zombie work, the unusual *Zombies on Broadway*.

Brains!

Despite the fact that only the most diehard of zombie cinema fans are even aware of *I Walked with a Zombie*, in 2007 it was awarded the fifth spot on *Stylus* magazine's list of the "Best Zombie Films of All Time." It's currently in the process of being transferred to and distributed on DVD. Until that time, it remains available in the public domain and may be found on Internet film archives and video-sharing sites such as YouTube. Recent online chatter indicates that exclusive rights were granted to an owning party. This means that once it's put back in production, it'll cease to be public domain. So watch it online while it's still free to all.

I Walked with a Zombie was released in 1943. To create the story, Lewton drew inspiration from a work of literature, Charlotte Bronte's *Jane Eyre*. Lewton and Tourneur shared a vision of a horror film that did not try to convince the audience that anything was or was not supernatural. Instead, they would simply present the audience with a situation and allow them to make up their own minds (as well as provoke what is perhaps the most common human phobia, the fear of the unknown).

A Canadian nurse named Betsy Connell (played by Frances Dee) took a nursing job for a wealthy sugar plantation family, the Hollands, on the Caribbean island of *Saint Sebastian*. Don't bother trying to locate the island on a map or online, because you won't find it. And if you are using most Internet search engines, it will take you hours of looking before you finally realize that there is no Caribbean island named Saint Sebastian (which is what happened when it was researched for this book). There are cities, townships, and provinces throughout the Caribbean by that name—but not a single island. Saint Sebastian is a fictional location that Lewton created in order to add a symbolic/spiritual/religious element to the storyline. Lewton used this imaginary island again in his second zombie film, *Zombies on Broadway*, but that time he changed the name of it to San Sebastian.

Mooooooaaaaaan...

Saint Sebastian is a Christian martyr who was executed twice (yes, twice) by Emperor Diocletian around 288 C.E. He joined the Roman Praetorian Guard, under violent anti-Christians Maximian and Diocletian. Sebastian didn't reveal his Christianity, and worked within Rome's infrastructure to convert others. Sebastian's faith was later uncovered. Diocletian bound him to a post and let soldiers use him for archery practice. When a widow, Irene of Rome, came to retrieve Sebastian's body, she found him *alive*—a chest full of arrows and none of them fatal. She took him home and cared for his wounds. After recovering, Sebastian openly jeered at Diocletian as he passed on the street. This time, Diocletian ordered his Praetorians to beat Sebastian to death on the spot. So Sebastian was martyred twice. A fitting icon for a zombie film.

Betsy arrived at the plantation to care for Jessica Holland (played by Christine Gordon), the wife of Paul Holland (played by Tom Conway), who owned and operated the family's plantation of Fort Holland. Paul also lived with his half-brother, the charming but *very* heavy-drinking Wesley Rand (played by James Ellison), and was frequently visited by his strong and confident mother, Mrs. Rand (she was mother to both men, but they have different fathers—Paul's father was from the Holland family, and Wesley was the son of their mother's second husband, Mr. Rand).

Brains!

It has been speculated that *I Walked with a Zombie* was the inspiration for the 2005 suspense film *Skeleton Key*, starring Kate Hudson. Both films are about young nurses who move into the homes of wealthy families in order to care for someone afflicted by a Voodoo curse. The film *Skeleton Key* is set in New Orleans, Louisiana, instead of on a fictional island in the Caribbean.

The first night Betsy stayed at Fort Holland, she awoke to what sounded like a woman crying. She looked outside to see Jessica Holland (her patient-to-be) entering a tower. She followed her, and when she came face-to-face with the woman, Betsy was frightened by the blank look on her face as she advanced to her. Betsy screamed, which brought Paul, Wesley, and some of the servants to the tower. They returned Jessica to bed and explained to Betsy that she had become ill not long ago and had been in this trancelike state ever since. The Holland estate courtyard had a fountain depicting the first execution of Saint Sebastian (he was executed twice because the first didn't quite take), bound to a post with multiple arrows sticking in his chest. The centerpiece/statue was taken from the prow of a slave ship, which Paul Holland later used to explain to Betsy the thought processes of the Haitians, who were the descendants of the slaves brought over on just such ships. "They cry when a baby is born—celebrate at funerals," he told her, and was fond of saying, when it comes to Haiti, "Everything good dies here."

The next day, Betsy met with Jessica's personal physician, who explained that the extreme fever of her illness (which he called "Tropical Fever") had damaged her spinal column and nervous system. As a result, she no longer had any will. "I think of her as a sleepwalker who can never be woken up," he told Betsy.

Through a series of events, some serious tension between Paul and Wesley became clear. Wesley at one point had an affair with Jessica, his brother's wife. When the two tried to run away together, Paul refused to let Jessica go (though it is never said, it is suggested that he may have been abusive, or at least used physical force to keep her from leaving).

Betsy refused to be content with just treating Jessica. She wanted to find a way to cure her. With the aid of Jessica's physician, and with Paul's permission, they tried administering an experimental and dangerous form of shock treatment, called "insulin shock," which was a real (and very risky) procedure that involved giving patients heavy injections of insulin that would put them in comas. Once in a comatose state, the patient was injected with a sudden and heavy dose of glucose. This was supposed to cause the body to experience a sudden rush of adrenaline, epinephrine, and endorphins. The idea was that this could "jump-start" a person who was in a trancelike or semi-catatonic state. By the 1960s, it was all but banned by the medical and psychiatric communities.

Finding nothing in conventional medicine that could help her patient, Betsy had her interest piqued when one of the Haitian servants at Fort Holland told her that a Voodoo *houngan* had brought an aunt of hers (who had gone mad after the death of her son) back from "the mindlessness." Despite the opposition of just about everyone, Betsy snuck Jessica out of Fort Holland and had the servant take her to the local *houngan*.

After a frightening journey through a labyrinthlike sugar cane field, they arrived at their destination. During the ceremony, Betsy was told to go alone to the back of the tent to meet the *houngan*. She was shocked to pull back the curtain to see Mrs. Rand sitting before her. Mrs. Rand (herself a trained physician) was the *houngan*. She explained that by claiming to be a *houngan* with supernatural powers, she was better able to get the locals to accept her medical treatments. She also told Betsy that nothing could be done for Jessica.

While the two of them talked, Jessica was still in the tent with the other Voodoo adherents. They decided to test her, and the saber-wielding ritual leader put his blade into her arm. She didn't bleed, so they wanted to do a blood ritual to test whether she was a zombie. They were about to take even more swords to her when Betsy and Mrs. Rand came in. Mrs. Rand told Betsy to hurry Jessica back to Fort Holland. Betsy's hopes of finding a cure through Voodoo were dashed. But the weirdness of this film had only just begun.

The locals were not happy that they had been denied the chance to test Mrs. Rand's zombie, as is customary of other *houngans*. The drumbeats intensified as the group descended on Fort Holland. They demanded that Jessica be handed over for a ritual test. Up until now, most of the white settlers had thought of Voodoo as just superstitious nonsense—something amusing and somewhat pitiful. Suddenly and violently, this view changed. One of the Haitians who led the ritual dances, called the *Sabreur* (basically, "Saberer," as in "one who wields a saber"), sent his tall and freaky-looking servant (who could be a zombie) named Carre-Four to Fort Holland with orders to bring Jessica back to the *humfort*, by force, if necessary. About this time, all hell broke loose.

The family discussed sending Jessica away to an asylum to calm the locals and protect her. Paul urged Betsy to book passage back to Canada as soon as possible. Then the tall, creepy figure of Carre-Four came bursting in. As he was about to seize Jessica, Mrs. Rand ordered him to stop. And, oddly enough, he did. She told him to go back to the *humfort*. And, rather surprisingly, he did exactly as she had commanded.

Due to all the local unrest, an official investigation was begun into the nature of Jessica's illness. The idea was to prove that she was *not* a zombie. But what happened next tossed that right out the window. Wesley started by accusing Paul of being responsible for Jessica's condition, and vice versa. Then Mrs. Rand spoke up … and dropped a bombshell on everyone.

Mrs. Rand said that at first she had only pretended to be the *houngan* to help her with her local patients. But that had changed on the night she had learned about the affair between Wesley and Jessica. When she had realized that Jessica was going to destroy her family, she claimed that her body became possessed by the snake god *Damballah* (see Chapter 1). This gave her the power to turn her adulterous daughter-in-law into a zombie, one of the living dead. No one believed her but Wesley. He immediately set out to find a way to reverse his mother's zombie curse. At one point, he asked Betsy if she would be willing to perform euthanasia and end Jessica's suffering. Betsy, of course, refused.

The *Sabreur*, however, was not done with the Hollands just yet. He came to Fort Holland personally, a wax doll resembling Jessica in his hand. He manipulated the doll, and soon Jessica came to the gate and let him in. Though the movie never says exactly why (one would assume that the *Sabreur* is causing all this), Wesley emerged from the house and pulled an arrow from the chest of the Saint Sebastian statue. The *Sabreur* stabbed the wax doll with a pin, and at the same moment Wesley drove the arrow straight through Jessica's broken heart. He picked her up and, as if in a trance, carried her out to the sea with empty eyes. The bodies of the two tragic lovers were found washed ashore the next day. They were brought back to Fort Holland, where Betsy (who, in the form of a voiceover throughout the film, had expressed her growing romantic feelings for Paul, which she had restrained because his wife still lived) was consoling Paul. With Paul's wife dead, she could finally express her love freely. This is an odd film, indeed, but certainly a good one.

The Least You Need to Know

◆ Most of the early zombie films dealt with Voodoo zombies, not the viral zombies with which we are now familiar.

◆ *White Zombie* is the first zombie film ever made, as well as one of the very first horror films with sound.

◆ While *White Zombie* is viewed as a classic by zombie fans, the Halperin brothers' follow-up zombie film, *Revolt of the Zombies*, is usually not.

◆ Some argue that the 1936 film *Ouanga*, and not *Revolt of the Zombies*, was actually the second zombie film ever made (and it very well may have been).

◆ If you watch *King of the Zombies* expecting a frightening zombie film, you will be disappointed.

◆ *I Walked with a Zombie* is set on the Caribbean island of Saint Sebastian, which does not actually exist.

Chapter 10

George A. Romero's "Dead"

In This Chapter

- ◆ The life and films of George A. Romero
- ◆ *Night of the Living Dead*, the film that started it all
- ◆ *The Crazies* and its influence on later viral-apocalypse films
- ◆ *Dawn of the Dead*, the rise of mass consumerism, and *Land of the Dead*
- ◆ Recent *Dead* films by George A. Romero
- ◆ The modern attempts to remake Romero's early films

George A. Romero is often referred to as the "Father of the Modern Zombie" and is widely viewed as the creator of modern zombie cinema. These titles are certainly well earned, considering that Romero has written and directed more zombie films than any other person in history, in addition to a multitude of other, nonzombie horror films. Romero's early zombie films set the standard for all that followed. Many of today's zombie filmmakers have been heavily influenced by Romero's works.

George A. Romero

George Andrew Romero was born on February 4, 1940, in New York City, to a Cuban American commercial artist (his father) and a Lithuanian immigrant (his mother). His introduction to filmmaking began during his education at Carnegie Mellon University in Pittsburgh. After his graduation in 1960, Romero began directing small segments for television.

Romero's first paid directing job, ironically enough, was for a short segment on the popular children's program *Mister Rogers' Neighborhood*. The part he directed was filming the process of Mr. Rogers' tonsillectomy. In an odd twist, this project somehow inspired Romero to pursue a career in horror films. And he attacked this new endeavor with great enthusiasm.

Romero assembled a group of friends, and together they founded their own movie studio, which they dubbed Image Ten Productions. Each person had to put up an equal share of the startup capital (around $10,000) to begin their first feature film—*Night of the Living Dead*. The script was written by John Russo and directed by George A. Romero. Little did they know that this movie would come to be viewed as one of the great classics of horror/zombie cinema. Unfortunately for Image Ten Productions, most of the films that followed were not successful.

Night of the Living Dead was created on an impressively meager budget of just over $100,000. For a feature film, even during the 1960s, this was a very low budget. But the film's storytelling and setting, in addition to its grainy, black-and-white film, made expensive special effects unnecessary. What makes its meager budget even more impressive is the fact that the movie grossed over $12 million in the United States, and more than $30 million worldwide. The sad truth, however, is that Romero saw little of this money. And due to seedy practices by the film's distribution company, Romero (and Image Ten Productions) lost the copyright to the film.

A film is required to have a copyright stamp on the title frame of the film prints in order for copyright to be maintained. Image Ten Productions had this, though under the original title they had given the movie, which was *Night of the Flesh Eaters*. The Walter Reade

Organization, which distributed the film, changed the title of the film to *Night of the Living Dead*. When they changed the title, they changed the title frame and did not put a copyright mark on it. As a result, *Night of the Living Dead* is now public domain. Despite the fact that Romero created the film, he no longer has exclusive rights to it. He doesn't like to be asked about this (which is understandable), but he has been quoted as often giving the simple answer, "Walter Reade ripped us off."

Brains!

It is a little-known fact that George A. Romero makes a cameo appearance as one of the corrections officers who guards the vicious criminal Hannibal Lecter's cell. After all, Romero's zombies have something in common with Lecter—they both like eating human flesh.

Though Romero is best known for his work in zombie movies, he also has a varied and long filmography of nonzombie films such as these:

- *The Crazies* (1973): A film about a virus that causes homicidal madness, and which is considered by many to have been the inspiration for the modern film of similar plot, *28 Days Later*

- *Knightriders* (1981): A film about men who compete in Medieval-style jousting, except on motorcycles

- *Creepshow* (1982): An anthology of frightening short films

- *Monkey Shines* (1988): An adaptation of the Stephen King novel of the same title, about a murderous monkey toy

- *Two Evil Eyes* (1990): A film adaptation of two short stories by Edgar Allan Poe

- *The Dark Half* (1993): Another adaptation of a Stephen King novel of the same title, about an author who discovers he has an evil doppelganger

- *Bruiser* (2000): Written and directed by Romero, a film about a man who is pushed around and disrespected his entire life, until one morning he awakens to find his face replaced by a blank white mask that alters his personality

These days, Romero has taken up residence in Toronto, Ontario, Canada. He has permanent Canadian residency, which he applied for shortly after filming *Land of the Dead* in Toronto back in late 2004 to early 2005. Since then, he also shot his 2007 film *Diary of the Dead* and his most recent (and, some speculate, his final) zombie film there. His latest film is titled *Survival of the Dead* (though the movie's title has changed from the original preproduction ... *Of the Dead* to *Island of the Dead* to the current title, so this may change by the time it's released). For more details on Romero's zombie films, just keep reading.

Night of the Living Dead (1968)

Many fans of zombie cinema consider Romero's *Night of the Living Dead* to be the progenitor of modern zombie cinema. Its release marks the birth of the entire genre of zombie films. First released in 1968, *Night of the Living Dead* was one of the most shocking horror films that American audiences had ever seen.

Set in rural Pennsylvania, *Night of the Living Dead* began with a young woman, Barbara (played by Judith O'Dea), being driven by her brother, Johnny (played by Russell Streiner), to visit the gravesite of their father. Johnny, with his leather driving gloves and smug, devil-may-care attitude, complained about having to waste a whole Sunday just to bring a wreath of flowers to the grave. A stereotypically fragile young woman, Barbara chastised Johnny for being so cold and disrespectful. This exchange of dialogue between them gives viewers the impression that Johnny is a bit of a "bad boy" (though by today's standards he probably doesn't measure up to such a title). They placed the wreath on the grave and Barbara offered a prayer, much to Johnny's annoyance.

As the two prepared to head back to their car, they spied a tall, strange-looking man moving slowly toward them. Johnny, ever the prankster, began spooking Barbara, pretending the man was a killer who was after them and delivering the legendary line (with atypical "spooky" tone of voice), "He's coming to *get* you, Barbara." Barbara feared that the man heard her brother and would be offended.

Brains!

Don't believe that a line as simple as "They're coming to *get* you, Barbara!" is legendary? Just try putting "coming to get you" or "they're coming to get you" (both without the "Barbara") into any Internet search engine, and you will find at least a handful of sites on the first page that reference the line from *Night of the Living Dead.*

Barbara, ever the polite young woman, approached the man to apologize for her brother's behavior. Unfortunately, he was a zombie and lunged at her. Johnny, hearing his sister scream, realized Barbara was in danger and came to her aid. During a short struggle with the zombie, Johnny was knocked down and cracked his head against a nearby tombstone. The zombie again turned for Barbara, who ran for the car in a panic.

When Barbara reached the vehicle, however, she realized that Johnny (whom she had abandoned, unconscious or possibly dead, back at the grave) had the keys. The zombie began to catch up to her, so Barbara took refuge inside the unlocked car (it was the 1960s, so unlocked cars were more common than today). The zombie soon reached the car and began clawing at the windows and bashing against the doors. Barbara, unable to start the car, instead put it in neutral, sending it rolling down an incline and away from the pursuing zombie.

Unfortunately, Barbara was a terrible driver (which could be due to her state of panic or just plain old poor driving skills). She ran off the road and collided with a tree at a relatively minimal speed, but it was enough to stop her momentum and bring her slow flight to a halt. She saw that the zombie was still coming, though from a longer distance, and again she took off on foot through the nearby woods.

Barbara's flight soon brought her to a rural farmhouse. She ran to it, screaming out for help. Inside, she found the phone dead (the zombie was shown walking through and breaking the flimsy phone cable). As she ventured upstairs, Barbara soon realized that the phone wasn't the only dead thing in the house, when she discovered a gnawed-upon corpse. Hysterical with fear, she began to flee the house. As she opened the door, however, she saw her pursuing zombie outside, now joined by another member of the walking dead.

Enter a New Kind of Hero

A truck soon sped up to the house, and a young African American man stepped out, tire iron in hand. He rushed up to Barbara and ushered her back inside the relative safety of the house. When the zombies began pelting the vehicle with rocks, however, he ventured back outside and dispatched both of them with his tire iron. While he was occupied with this, another zombie emerged from a closed door in the farmhouse. Barbara did not see him. The young man looked up just in time and came rushing inside. He took out the third zombie, shut the front door, and went to check the back. He found the back door open, with another half-dozen or so zombies lumbering toward it. He smacked the closest zombie in the face with the tire iron and secured the rear door.

With the danger averted for the moment, he tried asking Barbara questions. Unfortunately, she was nearly catatonic from the shock of what had happened. The young, tire iron–wielding African American's name was Ben (played by Duane Jones), and the truck he arrived in was running on fumes. He had originally stopped at the farmhouse because he saw that it had a gas pump out back. Unfortunately, the pump had a heavy lock. Ben searched every drawer and closet in the house, but the key was nowhere to be found. During his search, however, he found a lever-action rifle and a box of ammunition.

Ben knew that the mob of zombies at the rear of the house would soon reach them and start trying to get in. He also knew that he would need to buy some time to board up the doors and windows, so he immediately took action. He lit a fire in the home's center fireplace, then fashioned a torch by tearing curtains into strips and wrapping them around the end of a chair leg. Ben scooted a large reclining chair near the back door and doused it with lighter fluid. He lit the torch, opened the door, and shoved the chair onto the back porch. He lit up the chair with the torch and kicked the flaming piece of furniture into the backyard. The zombies shrieked and recoiled, showing that Ben had created a temporary barrier of fire between the zombies and the house, and offering the audience a valuable piece of information about a weakness of these living dead—they were afraid of fire.

Now that Ben had the back of the house secured, he began reinforcing the house, boarding up the doors and windows with anything he could find. Barbara, still in shock, wasn't much help. While Ben went to work, she sat on the couch staring at the walls. At this point, two men emerged from the one door that Ben had been unable to open. This scared the living daylights out of the now emotionally traumatized Barbara. Her screams brought Ben running, but he realized that the men were not zombies. Five other people had been in the house all along; they had barred themselves down in the basement. This is where things get problematic, and where the true point of Romero's film begins to unfold.

The people in the basement turned out to be Harry Cooper (a rather abrasive, high-strung, and self-centered individual), along with his wife, Helen, and daughter, Karen. They were accompanied by a young local couple, known in the film only by the first names Tom and Judy. Harry and his family had their vehicle turned over by a mob of zombies, and their daughter had been injured as they'd made their escape. Tom and Judy had been enjoying a day at the lake when they'd heard the reports on the radio. They had known the people who had lived in the house, so they'd headed there … only to find everyone dead. Cooper, being an overbearing, controlling, and relatively cowardly man, had ordered all of them down into the basement and had barred the door from the inside—without food, water, a radio, or a television (all of which could have been found in the house). When they'd heard Barbara screaming before, Cooper had not allowed anyone to open the door to help, claiming, "It could have been one of those things, for all I knew."

Man vs. Zombie, Man vs. Man

Romero's zombie movies, you see, are not actually about zombies at all. They are about us, about human beings and how we interact with one another. Romero used (and still uses) zombies as a device for social commentary, and a plethora of filmmakers and storytellers have followed this example ever since. *Night of the Living Dead* is not a movie about zombies, but about a group of human beings and how they react to one another during a time of crisis.

In Romero's debut zombie film, the cast of characters represented a diversity of social, economic, and racial groups of the 1960s:

◆ Barbara (and, although briefly, her brother Johnny): Your basic white Anglo-Saxon Protestants, most likely from the upper-middle class, judging from their expensive clothes and Johnny's nice car

◆ Harry, Helen, and Karen Cooper: White-collar middle class (also, it is somewhat implied that Harry physically abuses his wife)

◆ Tom and Judy: White, rural working class

◆ Ben: African American male; we are told nothing about his background (except for the events that brought him to the house), but judging from his clothing, intelligence, and demeanor, some believe Romero meant to imply that Ben is from the middle or upper-middle class, or at least well educated

I'm Boss Up Here

It didn't take long for a power struggle to commence between Ben and Cooper, who have very different (and conflicting) personalities. Cooper was a bully by nature, the kind of man who liked to bark orders at people. Ben, on the other hand, was not easily intimidated, a guy who thought things through and made his own decisions. It was a match made in hell. And Tom, a local young man who didn't have Ben's knack for asserting his opinions, found himself between them.

Cooper wasn't upstairs a few minutes before he started ordering everyone to go down into the basement. When Ben and Tom didn't immediately comply, he threatened to bar the door for good and permanently lock everyone out. Ben, however, realized that there was no way out of the basement and that it would only become a deathtrap if the zombies were to get in. Tired of being ordered around, Ben told Cooper, "You get the hell down in the cellar. You can be boss down there. *I'm* boss up here."

Cooper tried to take Barbara. Ben told him to stay away from her. Cooper then tried to lay claim to the radio and announced that he was taking it down to the basement. Ben, who had spent hours barricading the house without any assistance, refused to let Cooper take anything. "You stay away from her," Ben told Cooper. "And that goes for everything else that's up here, too. Because if I'm staying up here, I'm fighting for everything up here. And the radio and the food are part of what I'm fighting for." Before Cooper went back to the basement, Tom called for his girlfriend, Judy, to come up. Cooper fumed at this, saying, "You gonna let them get her, too?"

Cooper found himself in an unbearable situation for a man of his disposition. Bullying wasn't getting him anywhere, and he couldn't force Ben to do anything. As you may remember, Ben was in possession of the only gun. Coward that he was, Cooper went back into the basement and barred the door as Tom kept trying to reason with him that the best thing to do was to have everyone work together. "Let them stay up there," Cooper told his wife with an expression of arrogance. "We'll see who's right." Once Mrs. Cooper learned that there was a radio and television upstairs, however, she unbarred the door and headed upstairs (much to her husband's anger). Their injured daughter, Karen (yes, she had been bitten and infected), spent the entire movie in the basement.

Bad News and Best-Laid Plans

Everyone huddled around the television to hear the shocking news. The newsman delivered yet another historic Romero-film line, saying, "Persons who have recently died are returning to life and committing acts of murder." He also reported that a recent space satellite probe, which had been orbiting Venus, had been destroyed in space when an unusual amount of radiation had been detected. This radiation, however, had somehow reached Earth, perhaps from falling remains of the probe. Viewers were told to immediately soak any recently deceased body with gasoline and burn it.

The television broadcast also informed them that people were being advised to head immediately for government-established rescue stations, which had food, water, medical staff, and protection from the National Guard. A prompt at the bottom of the screen revealed that a rescue station had been set up in the neighboring town of Willard. Ben explained that his truck was out of gas. Cooper revealed that there was a large key ring in the basement. They found it and began forming a plan to make their escape.

Tom volunteered to drive the truck while Ben held back the zombies with his torch and rifle. Cooper threw Molotov cocktails from an upstairs window so they could reach the truck. Once they were in, he rushed back downstairs and locked the door (he was supposed to open it when they returned). From there, the plan went south.

To avoid spoiling the end for those who have not yet had the opportunity to view the film, let's conclude this section with a simple statement. When the dead walk the earth, humankind's greatest threat is humankind.

The Crazies (1973)

This section should begin with the concession that Romero's 1973 film *The Crazies* is not, technically, a zombie film. That is, the movie does not feature the flesh-eating living dead common to zombie films. However, this film is worthy of special mention due to its influence on a number of later zombie/viral apocalypse films.

Brains!

Some speculate that Romero's *The Crazies* may have inspired certain elements of American author Stephen King's epic viral apocalypse novel *The Stand*. The novel portrays the downfall of human civilization after a manmade "super-flu" virus is unleashed on the world, as well as those who survive it (both good and evil). *The Stand* was also adapted into a TV miniseries in 1994.

In the tiny burg of Evans City, Pennsylvania, people were beginning to act a little strange. The first of these unusual events was an arson case in which a local farmer, apparently consumed by dementia, set fire to his own barn for no reason whatsoever. And this was only the beginning. Soon, it was as if the entire town had gone mad.

It was soon disclosed to the viewer that a secret military research facility located nearby had accidentally unleashed a manmade virus that caused those infected to go insane, often violently. Evans City was immediately besieged by soldiers in full *NBC* gear. In order to contain the virus, as well as to keep the truth of it from being discovered by the general public, the soldiers had orders to shoot any infected civilians. Eventually, the soldiers' orders were upgraded to include shooting *any civilians they encountered.*

Moooooaaaaan...

NBC, in military terms, stands for Nuclear, Biological, and Chemical. "NBC gear" refers to equipment worn by personnel in order to avoid exposure and/or infection by nuclear, biological, or chemical agents. Such gear includes, but is not limited to: gas masks, "clean suits" (sometimes called "Gumby Suits" by soldiers because they are often constructed of green rubber material), and MARK I NAAK needles containing Atropine 2-Pam Chloride (a combination meant to jump-start the heart and block the body's absorption of the poisoning agent).

As Evans City fell into madness and chaos, David and Clank, two recently returned Vietnam veterans, realized that something was not quite right. David was a former Green Beret and Clank served in the Army's basic infantry. Along with David's pregnant girlfriend, a local nurse named Judy, the group attempted to make it out of the area. They soon learned that their homicidal neighbors were not the only ones they had to avoid. The three of them were taken prisoner by soldiers and, realizing they would soon be executed, escaped along with a teenage girl named Kathie and her father Artie. Now a group of five, they continued their escape.

As night fell, the group came upon a small patrol squad of soldiers. David and Clank ambushed them and managed to take one soldier alive. They interrogated him and learned the ghastly truth—the virus was now in the town's water supply, and in order to prevent it from spreading, the Pentagon had scrambled bombers equipped with nuclear weapons. They had a very small window to escape the area before it was turned into a nuclear wasteland. There was only one problem. The night before, Kathie, Artie, and Judy drank water from the faucets of a house in which they took shelter. David and Clank now had to contend with homicidal townspeople, armed soldiers, and their three increasingly deranged travel companions. How could any of them make it out of this alive?

Dawn of the Dead (1978)

Ten years after his debut with *Night of the Living Dead*, Romero returned to zombie cinema in 1978 with the film that many consider his masterpiece, *Dawn of the Dead*. Just as *Night of the Living Dead* is Romero's commentary on the societal chaos and racial tensions of the 1960s, *Dawn of the Dead* is his commentary on the rising consumerism, police brutality, and rampant commercialism that marked the 1970s. In relation to the first film, *Dawn of the Dead* is supposed to be set three weeks after *Night of the Living Dead*.

Dawn of the Dead opens in a television news station, with the film's heroine, Francine (played by Gaylen Ross), being startled awake as she napped in a corner. The newsroom around her was in a state of total chaos. As the program aired, members of the film crew were cursing and shouting at the man being interviewed (a government representative who was trying to explain that people who were dead or infected must be immediately exterminated). Many were abandoning their jobs, trying to get out while they could. Francine defied her boss and had their list of rescue stations taken off the air after she heard reports that more than half of them had been overrun and wiped out. Her boss complained about their ratings, saying that people would stop watching if the rescue stations weren't on the screen. "Without those rescue situations onscreen every minute," he barked at her, "people won't watch us. They'll tune out." Francine asked him (while speaking on an intercom that could be heard on the air), "Are you willing to murder people by sending them out to stations that have closed down?" His reply: "I want that list up on the screen every minute we're on the air." Hearing this, everyone in the control room walked out. The boss yelled out to a police officer who was guarding the exit to stop the people trying to leave. The officer just rolled his eyes, grabbed his coat, and walked out the door.

Soon Francine's boyfriend, Steven, a chopper pilot for the news station, arrived. He told her to meet him on the roof and said he would pick her up in the chopper so they could escape the city. At first, Fran protested, but then she learned that the station was about to be switched over to the Emergency Broadcast System anyway.

The film then moved to another main character, a police officer named Roger (played by Scott Reiniger). The police had a building in the housing projects surrounded, with a wanted gang leader and his followers inside. They stormed the building to learn that the tenants had boarded up certain sections with their recently reanimated dead. When one bigoted officer, who had been spouting racial slurs, went insane and started shooting anyone he encountered, Roger tried to restrain him. Another officer, his face covered by a gas mask, ordered Roger to get away from the maniac. Roger was thrown to the ground, and the other officer shot the homicidal cop. None of the other officers said a word about it.

Roger headed to a lower-level laundry room, trying to clear the tear gas from his face with water, when the gas mask–wearing cop confronted him. He removed the mask, revealing that he was a very large and intimidating African American. His name was Peter (played by Ken Foree). They cleared the air, and Roger explained that if anyone asked, he "didn't see anything." Roger, it turned out, was a friend of Stephen, who had asked him to join them on the chopper. He invited Peter to tag along. Realizing that staying was only likely to get him killed, Peter agreed.

The four joined up and took the chopper out of the city. They got a small amount of fuel at an abandoned air depot, where they ran into a few zombies. They eventually reached Pittsburgh, with no new fueling stations in sight. They all needed rest, so when they saw a large shopping mall, they landed on the roof. The group soon realized that if they cleared the mall and secured the doors, they could live safely in the mall for quite some time. They blocked the entrances with cargo trucks, but during this, Roger was bitten on the leg. They then locked all the doors and, after raiding the mall's gun store, went "on a hunt" as Peter called it. During this time, Francine was discovered to be pregnant. Peter asked Stephen whether they wanted to keep the baby, explaining that he knew how to do a wire hanger abortion (don't worry, they didn't do it).

For some time, they lived in the mall. Roger's condition deteriorated over time. He was soon delusional from fever and bedridden. As he lay dying, he told Peter, "I'm gonna try not to come back." Unfortunately, trying didn't work, and Peter had to put a bullet in his friend's head. The group soon realized that staying in the mall was not living, it was just waiting to die. They began packing up supplies, and Fran started learning how to fly the chopper. The sound of a chopper, however, brought more to their doorstep than just zombies.

An army of looter-raider bikers saw the chopper and decided that they wanted the mall for themselves. They called on the radio, claiming friendship. Peter ordered Stephen and Francine to stay off the radio. The raiders, however, had made up their minds and, soon enough, moved one of the trucks. They came crashing through the doors, unknowingly giving hundreds of zombies a way to follow them in. A firefight ensued between the gang members and Peter and Stephen. Peter headed for the safe room to meet up with Fran, but Stephen was trapped in an elevator and bitten by a zombie. He turned and began leading the other zombies to the hidden room. As for the gang of looters, they discovered their mistake too late and were overrun by the undead. None of them made it out of the mall alive.

In the end, Peter sent Fran to the chopper on the roof. He had planned to use himself as bait so she could escape. He put a small pistol to his head and let the zombies come at him. At the last second, however, he had a change of heart and used the one bullet on a zombie. He went kung fu on the zombies and made a dash for the roof. He got to the chopper and escaped with Fran. They didn't know where they were going or how far their remaining fuel would take them ... but as they flew into the distance, they were both smiling.

Day of the Dead (1985)

The next installment of Romero's *Dead* series, *Day of the Dead*, continues Romero's trend of social commentary. This film looks at the ever-present conflicts that exist between science and the military, the rational and powerful, those with brains and those with guns. How much time is supposed to have passed between *Dawn of the Dead* and *Day of the Dead* is a matter of much debate among Romero fans.

Romero is legendary for giving conflicting answers on this question. Many fans have tried to look for clues in the film. Some point to a field of marijuana plants that are being grown, claiming that such plants would takes months to grow to such a height. However, even Romero claims that this wasn't done to establish any timeline. Others point to the ghostly, zombie-ridden city that a helicopter full of soldiers visit in search of survivors. In all honesty, it is likely that *Day of the Dead* occurs quite some time later, probably anywhere from six months to a few years.

Aside from the opening scene, most of the movie takes place in an underground bunker that the military has adapted into a lab so that a group of scientists can try to find a solution to the zombie epidemic. They also left a platoon of soldiers in the bunker to protect them. By this point, however, the soldiers were becoming impatient with the scientists for their lack of results. Of course, this impatience was largely due to the fact that a lot of the soldiers were bitten or killed while trying to round up "specimens" for the scientists' experiments. Their commanding officer had recently died, leaving in charge his much younger, arrogant, and short-tempered second-in-command officer.

When the soldiers learned that the chief scientist had been feeding his "specimens" the flesh of dead soldiers (which he kept in a cold lock), the new commanding officer flipped out and shot him. One female scientist, a Caribbean chopper pilot, and an Irish electrician made a mad dash for the chopper to escape the wrath of the soldiers. To cover their escape, an infected soldier (who had been having a romantic but turbulent relationship with the scientist) used himself as bait and led hundreds of zombies into the base by way of a cargo elevator, and then disabled the control. One zombie specimen, affectionately referred to as "Bub," had learned to shoot a pistol and took revenge on the officer who had shot his trainer/scientist. He shot the officer and then left him to be ravaged by a horde of zombies. As the officer was ripped in half and the zombies began to chow down on his intestines, he delivered yet another famous Romero film line: "Choke on 'em! Choke on 'em!"

The escaping trio landed on a deserted island, and one might assume they lived happily ever after.

Land of the Dead (2005)

Romero's *Land of the Dead* installment of the series takes place in the future, well after the world has been overrun by zombies. On the private, manmade island complex of Fiddler's Green, however, it was business as usual. During the last days of the zombie apocalypse, members of the wealthy elite used their financial means to secure Fiddler's Green, thus becoming the new rulers of a modern feudal empire. The ruling elite lived self-indulgent lives. They shopped, dined in fine restaurants, and lived in luxurious high-rise suites. The remaining survivors were allowed to live within the barricade and moat that separated Fiddler's Green from the outside. However, they were not allowed inside the city itself. They lived in abject poverty, the only escape from which was working for the elite ruling class as servants, soldiers/guards, or raiders.

The raiders were the lifeblood of Fiddler's Green, venturing out into the surrounding zombie-ridden town in search of needed food and supplies. They were paid for their services, but little of what they looted ended up in the hands of anyone but their rich employers. The flagship weapon of the raiders was an armored behemoth of a vehicle called "Dead Reckoning." It had everything—heavy machine guns, explosives, even long-range missile launchers. It was equipped to shoot fireworks into the night sky, which for years had been used as a distraction during raiding parties. The zombies simply stood and looked at the sky while the raiding party barreled through a town. One new member of the crew remarked, "I thought this was going to be a battle. This is a massacre."

The raiders were under the leadership of Riley (played by Simon Baker), who was also the chief of Dead Reckoning's crew. Riley hated Fiddler's Green, as well as the rich men who ran it. He finally had a working vehicle and planned to leave Fiddler's Green behind and hand off leadership of the raiders to his second-in-command, a cocky fellow named Cholo (played by John Leguizamo). Cholo, however, had other plans. He thought that since he had saved enough money, and performed enough dirty deeds for the elite, he'd be allowed to "buy in" to Fiddler's Green and live inside the city. When he was turned away, however, Cholo's mind turned to revenge. He and the rest of the crew hijacked Dead Reckoning and threatened to destroy Fiddler's Green with its long-range missiles if a hefty ransom was not paid.

The elite class was led by a man named Kaufman (played by Dennis Hopper). Kaufman had Riley's vehicle "misplaced" and offered to give him a vehicle and supplies if he would retrieve Dead Reckoning from Cholo. Riley accepted the mission because he had no other choice. He headed out with his sidekick, Charlie, a facially scarred and mentally challenged man who more than made up for his shortcomings with marksmanship ability. If they could not reach Cholo in time, everyone in Fiddler's Green was in danger. And that wasn't the only problem.

Riley had noticed that certain zombies had begun resuming behaviors from their lives, and some even seemed to communicate as if they could think. This became a problem when one exceptional zombie led an army of angry zombies to Fiddler's Green. It's safe to say that Fiddler's Green will never be the same.

Diary of the Dead (2007)

In 2007, Romero updated his vision of a zombie-infested world with *Diary of the Dead*. This installment of the *Dead* series goes back to the beginning of the timeline and follows a group of college film students during the outbreak of the zombie virus. While filming his final college project, a stereotypical mummy-type horror movie, film student Jason Creed found himself making a much different kind of project. As the world went insane, Jason began filming a documentary of the events that unfolded around himself and the rest of his student film crew as they fought their way across a zombie-ridden Philadelphia.

When the reports first began, some of the students thought it was a hoax (especially the makeup artist, Tony). Enough of them, however, were freaked out enough for the filming session to be called off. Jason and the others headed back to Pitt (University of Pittsburgh) to retrieve his girlfriend, Debra. As they drove away from campus to take her home in the film trailer, they came across an accident and several zombies converged on their vehicle. The driver, a very religious young girl named Mary, ran several of them down with the vehicle. Overcome by guilt because she believed she had killed three people, Mary shot herself when they stopped to rest. However, she was still alive. They rushed her to a rural hospital, where the situation wasn't much better. The group used her gun to shoot their way clear of a hospital full of zombies. Mary died as they unsuccessfully searched for a doctor.

They arrived at Debra's house to find that her entire family had become reanimated corpses. With nowhere left to go, the group decided to join up with a friend from their film project, Ridley, who lived in a mansion in rural Philadelphia with his affluent family. When they arrived, however, the girl who went with him, Francine, and his family members were nowhere to be found. To make matters worse, Ridley had lost his mind and failed to inform them that they were all now zombies. He dragged them all to the pool, getting himself bitten in the process. In the end, only a handful of them were able to secure themselves safely in the home's panic room. Even Jason was lost, being bitten because he could not stop filming. He lay on the ground, bleeding from the neck, and said, "Shoot me." His girlfriend pointed his camera at him and blew his head off.

Survival of the Dead (2010)

During preproduction, *Survival of the Dead* was given the simple title … *Of the Dead*. For a time, it was going to be called *Island of the Dead* because the movie is set on small Plum Island (located off the coast of Delaware), but in the end, Romero chose *Survival of the Dead* as the film's official title. The film was screened at a number of film festivals in 2009 and is slotted for release in U.S. theaters sometime in 2010.

The movie deals with a group of isolated survivors who have taken refuge on Delaware's Plum Island, allowing them to live in a relatively zombie-free environment. However, the island has long been home to two feuding families, the O'Flynns and Muldoons. When the world ended, they turned the island into a war zone. When the infection reaches the island, however, bringing zombies and survivors alike to their doorsteps, the two families must put

Brains!

Survival of the Dead and Land of the Dead are the only two Romero films that are not supposed to be set in Philadelphia.

aside their differences to face the common undead enemy. If they do not, the alternative is destruction.

Remaking Romero

George A. Romero is one of the most widely remade filmmakers in the world. To avoid confusion, here is a list of the most commonly known Romero film remakes:

◆ *Night of the Living Dead* (1990): Directed by Tom Savini.

◆ *Night of the Living Dead 3D* (2006): Most zombie fans agree that this film, directed by Jeff Broadstreet, is the worst Romero film remake in history.

◆ *Dawn of the Dead* (2004): Directed by Zack Snyder and released by Strike Entertainment.

◆ *Day of the Dead* (2008): Directed by Steve Miner. About the only thing this "remake" has in common with the original Romero film is its title.

◆ *The Crazies* (2010): Directed by Breck Eisner, this highly anticipated remake of Romero's main nonzombie classic released by Overture is scheduled for release sometime in 2010.

The Least You Need to Know

◆ While George A. Romero is famous for being the founder of the modern zombie genre, he has directed a number of nonzombie film projects.

◆ The first films of Romero's *Dead* series follow a steady timeline.

◆ *Diary of the Dead* returns to the beginning of the timeline (though in the modern decade), and *Survival of the Dead* takes place outside of any set timeline.

◆ George A. Romero is one of the most widely remade filmmakers in history, though not all the remakes are good.

Chapter 11

The Modern Zombie Cinema Canon

In This Chapter

- ◆ The most common (non-Romero) movies of the "zombie cinema canon"
- ◆ The romantic comedy (with zombies) *Shaun of the Dead*
- ◆ *Dance of the Dead*'s high school angst in the zombie apocalypse
- ◆ The nonzombies of *28 Days Later*
- ◆ The many faces of *Resident Evil*
- ◆ The recent success of the films *Dead Snow* and *Zombieland*

When it comes to the canon of zombie cinema, meaning those films which are considered the basis of zombie fandom, it is a given that all of Romero's zombie films are included. What follows in this chapter is a summarization of the non-Romero films that make up the zombie cinema canon.

Resident Evil Series

When the movie *Resident Evil*, based loosely on the video game of the same name (see Chapter 13), was released in 2002, it was the first zombie film to be made in nearly a decade. The movie's main heroine was a woman named Alice (played by Milla Jovovich) who awakened at the beginning of the film in her shower with no memory of who she was or how she came to be there. Moments later, a special paramilitary/mercenary unit came crashing into the house.

Brains!

> Critics aren't always right. Acclaimed movie critic Roger Ebert gave the film a negative review. However, it grossed over $100 million at the box office.

Alice was soon told by the leader of the unit that she was a special agent for the powerful Umbrella Corporation and that it had been her task to protect the house, which served as an alternate entrance to a secret underground laboratory called The Hive. The Hive was located deep beneath the nearby urban area of Raccoon City. For reasons unknown, the facility's artificial intelligence security system had sealed all the staff members inside and killed them.

Brains!

> The original title of the movie was supposed to be *Resident Evil: Ground Zero*, and was at first scripted as a prequel to the video games. However, the title was changed due to similarities with the name given to the sight of the 9/11 terrorist attacks on the World Trade Center. The original script also had the female characters Alice and Rain (Michelle Rodriguez) as the leaders of the special military unit tasked with containing an outbreak of the zombie T-Virus.

Apparently, someone had recently stolen a vial of a potent viral weapon called the T-Virus and, in the process, released it into the facility. The main result of infection by the T-Virus was the reanimation of dead tissue. The "Red Queen," which was the name of The Hive's AI system, realized that the only way to contain the infection was to seal all doors and kill everyone inside.

Alice was not alone when the military unit arrived. Another man was also in the house, and he identified himself as officer Matthew Addison (played by Eric Mabius). The team checked him out on the police database, but he claimed that he had just transferred and wasn't yet in the system. They handcuffed him and decided to bring him along. The team led Alice and Matt to an underground train that could take them to The Hive. On the train, they found yet another survivor. He, like Alice, was suffering from amnesia (which we learn was a side effect of the Red Queen's release of a knockout/nerve gas). This man was Spence (played by James Purefoy), and Alice recognized him from pictures she had seen back in the mansion.

Brains!

Milla Jovovich was born in the Ukraine in 1975. She came to the United States and began modeling at the age of 11 after being featured in *Revlon* magazine's 1986 list of "Most Unforgettable Women in the World" (impressive, considering she was still only a child). In addition to playing Alice in the *Resident Evil* series, Jovovich's film career has consisted of many action roles in such movies as *The Fifth Element* and *Ultraviolet,* making her an icon of horror/sci-fi. In recent years, VH1 crowned Jovovich with the title of "Reigning Queen of Kicking Butt."

Once at The Hive side of the train line, the team planned to bypass the security and infiltrate the facility. Their plan was to shut down the Red Queen and reboot the entire system. The Red Queen made herself visible as a holograph, taking on the voice and appearance of a young girl. They reached the Red Queen's chamber and ignored the computer's pleas to not shut her down. While heading down the corridor to the main chamber, four members of the team were trapped inside and cut to shreds by a grid of powerful lasers while their tech expert, Kaplan, tried to shut it down. He succeeded, but not soon enough to save his diced-up teammates.

Kaplan and Alice succeeded in reaching the main chamber. They shut down the Red Queen and rebooted the system. Just before shutting down, the Red Queen ominously told them, "You are all going to die down here." Unfortunately, the Red Queen was telling the truth. Rebooting the system unlocked all the doors in the facility. This freed the hundred or so reanimated staff members, who now wandered the facility in search of victims. The battle for survival was on.

Alice and Kaplan rendezvoused with the rest of the team, most of whom didn't fare too well when they suddenly found themselves surrounded by a horde of homicidal zombies. Rain (played by Michelle Rodriguez) was bitten numerous times and infected (though she doesn't turn until nearly the end of the film, because most of her bites are to her hands and forearms). Alice and Matt were separated from the team in the chaos. The film later reveals that Matt was not a police officer, but an environmental activist who was trying to get evidence that the Umbrella Corporation had been creating biological and chemical weapons. His sister, Lisa, who was assisting Matt, had managed to infiltrate the facility before she had been killed and reanimated by the T-Virus (and killed by Alice) when the Red Queen went homicidal. The plan had been for Lisa to smuggle out a sample of the T-Virus, and at first Matt believed that her contact in the facility must have betrayed her. Alice began having flashbacks that made her realize she had been Lisa's inside contact, and at first she feared that she had been the one who had betrayed the woman.

The group soon reunited in the Red Queen's control room. Alice turned her back on and Kaplan bypassed the system so that Alice could use the threat of "frying her" permanently to keep the AI from harming them. The Red Queen temporarily agreed to aid the team in their escape, since her only other option was oblivion. The survivors began to make their way through the facility's maintenance tunnels. Unfortunately, they found them crawling with zombies. Rain was bitten again, and Kaplan found himself completely cut off from the others. Surrounded by zombies, he was isolated on a flimsy ventilation tube. The others had no choice but to leave him behind and head for the train that would take them back to the mansion.

With an army of undead zombies and mutant monsters between them and safety, the few remaining survivors had to battle to escape The Hive before they were sealed inside it … permanently. The film ends on a cliffhanger, with Alice and Matt captured by Umbrella scientists, which directly led to the opening events in the second film in the series.

Resident Evil: Apocalypse

Resident Evil: Apocalypse, the second film of the series, was released in 2004. The film begins with a team being sent to reopen The Hive.

The team was attacked by the zombies in the facility, and the virus was unleashed into Raccoon City. In response, the Umbrella Corporation had created a solid perimeter wall around the entire city and trapped everyone (infected and uninfected both) inside. Alice (still played by Milla Jovovich), regained her memory and began gearing up for a fight.

Raccoon City police officer Jill Valentine (a character from the original video game) was recently framed in a cover-up by Umbrella for killing zombies. She reached the checkpoint at the perimeter wall, where Umbrella was screening people one by one before letting them leave the city. A gigantic crowd had formed by the time an Umbrella representative ordered them all to return to their homes. When no one complied, he threatened that they would open fire and began counting down. Valentine and the other police officers tried to get the civilians to move away from the wall. The countdown reached zero, and the Umbrella mercenaries opened fire on the crowd.

The film follows Alice, Jill Valentine, and a group of other survivors. They were joined later by an Umbrella mercenary, Carlos (played by Jared Harris), who was abandoned by his own employers. Together they must try to find some way out of Raccoon City before Umbrella has it "sanitized," all the while being pursued by a monstrous behemoth call "Nemesis." To "sanitize" Raccoon City, the Umbrella Corporation planned to unleash a nuclear weapon on Raccoon City to destroy the virus and cover up their activities. They were soon helped by an Umbrella scientist, Dr. Ashford (who we later learn was also the creator of the T-Virus), who enlisted them to save his daughter, still trapped in the city. The group managed to save the girl and find their way to a chopper. However, things didn't go smoothly.

The survivors reached the chopper, only to find out that the whole thing was an ambush. Major Cain of Umbrella had been tapping the computer communications of Dr. Ashford from the beginning. Cain ordered Alice to fight the giant monster, Nemesis. She refused, so Cain shot Dr. Ashford, then pointed the gun at the others and explained he would kill them if she didn't fight. Alice fought a tough battle against Nemesis and won, driving him back into a piece of sharp metal. As she did so, however, she looked into his eyes and realized that Nemesis was actually Matt Addison (the only other survivor from the original film).

Cain ordered Alice to finish off Nemesis/Matt, but she refused. Her refusal seemed to cause Matt to recognize the situation for what it was. He turned on the Umbrella forces, and a firefight ensued. Nemesis was killed in the battle, but the survivors made it to the chopper (with Major Cain in custody). A horde of zombies converged beneath the chopper and tossed Cain out, causing him to break his ankle. Cain took his sidearm and attempted to commit suicide, but found he was out of ammo. In a moment of poetic justice, a zombified Dr. Ashford crawled on him and took a bite as the other zombies descended for a tasty flesh buffet.

The survivors flew like the wind to escape from the 5-kiloton tactical nuke that soon detonated over Raccoon City. The bomb destroyed the city and sent a blast wave speeding outward. The helicopter was soon hit, and a piece of metal went flying toward Dr. Ashford's daughter. Alice jumped in front of it and the metal went through her chest. After this, we see flashing images of the helicopter's crash, with Alice fading in and out of consciousness.

The film once again ends on a cliffhanger, and the final scene shows Alice once more in the custody of Umbrella scientists. With the help of friends, she escaped yet again. However, it was obvious that something in her had been changed. Umbrella had done something to Alice. What they had done, however, remains unknown at the film's end.

Resident Evil: Extinction

The third installment of the series, *Resident Evil: Extinction*, was released in September 2007. We learn that Umbrella's use of a nuclear weapon to sanitize the Raccoon City outbreak failed. The T-Virus spread throughout the world. To make matters worse, the T-Virus was adaptive. It started killing more than just people, and it soon wiped out nearly every living thing on the planet ... even plant life.

The movie begins in the not-too-distant future, in a post-zombie-apocalyptic world with fuel, food, and water in short supply. The few human survivors banded into convoys that stay in motion, thus preventing the zombies from zeroing in on and surrounding them.

The Umbrella Corporation, despite the situation, remained active. From their underground facilities all over the world, they continued to perfect the T-Virus and were trying to find a solution to the bleak situation they found themselves in. They also continued what they called "Project Alice," using clones made from Alice's DNA. Meanwhile, they were hoping to locate the real Alice using surveillance satellites.

Speaking of Alice, she had separated herself from the other survivors. She rode alone through the zombie wasteland on a motorcycle, doing her best to stay out of sight when one of Umbrella's satellites passed overhead. At night she listened to her radio scanner, hoping to locate survivors and eavesdropping on the nearby human convoy. While looting an abandoned gas station, Alice found a diary that said the infection hadn't reached Alaska and that a colony of survivors was living there. One night, when her telekinetic powers got out of control, Alice accidentally trashed her motorcycle and so had to hook up with the convoy.

Carlos and T. J. (two survivors from the previous movie) had joined up with a convoy of human survivors led by Claire Redfield (a character from the game, played by Ali Larter). The survivors came upon an abandoned hotel, and while they were clearing it of zombies, T. J. was bitten and infected. No one saw him get bitten, however, and he didn't tell anyone. They decided to make camp for the night and sleep in their vehicles next to the hotel. They awoke the next morning to a flock of infected crows. The crows attacked the convoy, and several members of the group were killed. All seemed lost until Alice appeared and, using her new powers, set the sky on fire and incinerated all the infected birds.

Alice shared the diary with Carlos and Claire, and the members of the convoy voted to make an attempt to reach the Alaskan convoy (which may not even have existed). To get there, however, they needed fuel and supplies. The only place left that might have had what they needed was Las Vegas, Nevada, which, at last look, was crawling with zombies.

When they reached Vegas, however, they found that the infected crows had picked the city clean of zombies. However, they were greeted by a cargo container of new-and-improved zombies created by a revised version of the T-Virus. To make matters worse, the infected T. J. died and reanimated, turning on the others. The zombies nearly wiped out the entire convoy, and Alice was rendered paralyzed when Umbrella used its satellite linkup to "shut her down." Somehow she was able to overcome their control and short out the satellite. She killed the Umbrella agents, but the scientist Dr. Isaacs (from the end of the previous film), in charge of the experiment, escaped (but not before being bitten by one of his own altered zombies). He went back to his lab and began repeatedly injecting himself with the antivirus. He was shot by a fellow Umbrella agent but immediately reanimated and began to mutate uncontrollably. He wreaked havoc on the lab and turned on everyone.

Meanwhile, Alice and the others regrouped. They decided to storm the nearby Umbrella facility and steal a chopper to take them to Alaska. Carlos, who was bitten during the fight in Vegas, sacrificed himself to give the others a way into the facility. He drove the convoy's tanker, full of fumes, through the legion of zombies that surrounded its gates and laid it over. He then lit a bomb that created a huge gas explosion that blasted a clearing through the undead. The others sped through the opening and reached the chopper. Alice, however, did not go with them. She stayed behind to put an end to Umbrella's operations and kill the mutating Dr. Isaacs. Just before entering the facility, Alice found a mass grave in which she found dozens of dead clones of her.

In the lab, Dr. Isaacs had mutated into a monstrous figure. He had killed everyone else in the facility, save the White Queen, an updated version of The Hive's Red Queen in the first film. The White Queen realized that Alice was the only one strong enough to stop Isaacs, so she agreed to let her into the lab. But the White Queen also said she wouldn't let her out until Isaacs was destroyed. Alice fought a terrible battle against the mutant Isaacs, but in the end killed him … and in the process discovered one of her Alice clones in a stasis capsule. Now that Isaacs's body had been consumed and transformed by the new strain of the T-Virus, was Alice strong enough to bring him down and finally deliver true justice upon the remaining leaders of Umbrella for the crimes they had committed against humankind?

What comes next? Only another movie can tell us. There are rumors that another movie is in the works, but only time will tell.

28 Days Later: Not-Quite-Zombies

28 Days Later, though considered by many to be a part of the zombie canon, is not technically a zombie film. Released in 2002, this British film was directed by Danny Boyle and written by Alex Garland. The virus in this film, generally referred to as the "rage virus," did not bring the dead to life. Instead, it caused those infected by it to become overwhelmed with extreme homicidal rage against anyone not infected.

The virus was released into the world when one night a group of well-intentioned animal-rights activists broke into the Cambridge Primate Research Facility. They found the chimpanzee cages and, despite the warnings of a resident scientist that they were infected with "rage," set one free. It attacked them all, infecting the activists and the scientist.

Brains!

Many people have speculated that *28 Days Later* may have been inspired by the George A. Romero film *The Crazies*. Like *28 Days Later*, Romero's *The Crazies* is about a virus that caused those infected by it to be overcome with insanity and rage.

The main story of the film begins 28 days later, when a man named Jim (played by Cillian Murphy) came out of a coma in St. Thomas Hospital. He left the hospital and ventured out into the streets of London, which at first appeared to be completely deserted. Soon enough, however, Jim came upon some people—some infected people—who then began chasing him. He was lucky enough to be saved by a pair of tough survivors, Selena (played by Naomi Harris) and Mark (Noah Huntley), who took him to their subterranean hiding place. They explained to Jim that during his coma, the rage virus had spread throughout the world and turned nearly the entire population of the planet into mindless killing machines.

Brains!

28 Days Later was a hit, and is considered a classic among post-apocalyptic films. It was followed up with a higher-budget, mainstream sequel *28 Weeks Later*. Though it had a bigger budget and more Hollywood backing, the sequel did not come close to matching the status of its predecessor.

Selena and Mark accompanied Jim to the home of his parents, where he learned that both his mother and father had committed suicide. They took refuge there for the night but were attacked by several infected people. Mark was cut during the fight, meaning he was likely infected. He begged for his life as Selena killed him mercilessly with a machete. Jim was shocked at first, but Selena explained that the virus was the most infectious ever seen … and she also explained that she would kill him without hesitation if she thought he was infected.

The next day, they traveled the city and discovered two other survivors—a man named Frank (played by Brendan Gleeson) and his teenage daughter, Hannah (played by Megan Burns). They had barricaded their block of deserted flats, and Frank, wearing a suit of full body armor, had been able to kill any stragglers. They stayed the night with Frank and Hannah, and the next morning Frank confided in Jim that they were running low on supplies.

Frank also told Jim that he had been receiving a prerecorded broadcast from a military outpost near Manchester. In the broadcast, they were claiming to have an answer to the infection, as well as food, protection, and medical attention. Frank had a vehicle, his taxicab, and the group decided to make a run for the Manchester outpost.

When the group reached the blockade to the outpost, however, they found it deserted. The only thing there was a corpse lying on an upper crow's nest. Unfortunately, a drop of blood from the corpse hit Frank in the eye as he looked up, infecting him. Shots seemed to come from nowhere, killing him. They found that the soldiers were watching them from a concealed position. The soldiers commandeered the taxicab and brought Jim, Selena, and the heartbroken Hannah to the Manchester outpost.

What they found in Manchester was not what they had expected. There was no cure and few supplies. The outpost was nothing more than a bunch of rogue soldiers who had barely managed to hold out. Worse, the commanding officer had promised that he would get his men some females for "entertainment." Their so-called "answer" to the infection was to wait until the infected starved to death and, in the meantime, use the women, more or less, to make babies. Too late did they learn that this is what they had in store for Selena and Hannah. Jim, along with a soldier who wasn't going along with his unit's "answer," were restrained and sentenced to execution. In this moment they also learned, however, that the rest of the world had not been entirely infected. In fact, the entire island of Great Britain had been closed off for quarantine. But the virus had not spread to the rest of the world.

As his executioners argued about how they were going to kill him (with a knife or a bullet), Jim bounded over a wall and escaped. He headed back and lured the commander, West, and one of the soldiers out to the compound's blockade. He then headed for the compound and released Mailer, a soldier from the unit who was infected and had been kept chained up for "observation."

Jim fought his way through the compound in a bloody and daring rescue. He saved Selena a moment before she was about to be raped by a sadistic corporal. He so savagely killed the soldier that for a moment she wasn't sure whether Jim was infected. She held up a machete for a few moments, and Jim commented that she hesitated. As they kissed, Hannah came up from behind and hit Jim on the head with a vase, believing him to be either infected or one of the rapist soldiers.

As they made a run for the taxicab, West emerged and shot Jim in the stomach. Hannah jumped into the cab and backed it up toward West, forcing him to the front door of the compound and right into the arms (and teeth) of the infected Mailer. The others got in the taxicab and drove away from the compound. They rushed Jim to a hospital, where Hannah managed to remove the bullet and save Jim's life.

Brains!

> In one alternate ending to the film, the idea was that Jim would still be shot and taken to the hospital. However, he would die from his wounds despite Selena's efforts to save him. In the end, this ending was thought to be a bit too grim, considering all the violence and tragedy that had preceded it. In the original theatrical release, this ending followed by the words "What if ..." was run after the credits.

Jim woke up 28 days later, still recovering from his wounds, but this time in a cottage in the country. Jim stepped outside and found Selena and Hannah sewing together giant pieces of cloth. They worked together to lay out the recent, final piece of a giant banner that read "HELLO." A military jet suddenly passed overhead, and as they waved to it, the camera moved to a shot of a nearby road, where the infected were dying of starvation. The film ended with Selena saying, "Do you think they saw us this time?"

Shaun of the Dead

Perhaps no other film has done more to bring zombies back into the mainstream of pop culture than the 2004 British film *Shaun of the Dead*. The film was directed by Edgar Wright, who also co-wrote the script with Simon Pegg (who plays Shaun). Both Pegg and Wright were big fans of the zombie films of George A. Romero, and many of the one-liners in their film are, in fact, tributes to lines from his movies.

Brains!

Simon Pegg and Edgar Wright both played zombies in the George A. Romero film *Land of the Dead*. They are the zombies who are chained to a wall for the amusement of living humans, who take novelty pictures beside them.

The film follows a young Englishman named Shaun (Simon Pegg), a 29-year-old appliance store salesman who had done little to nothing with his life since college. His life had pretty much been the same routine for years—going to work, playing video games with his flatmate/sidekick Ed (played by Nick Frost), and spending his evenings at the Winchester, the local pub. His girlfriend, Liz (played by Kate Ashfield), grew tired of Shaun's lack of ambition. She gave him an ultimatum to start doing different things with her. He agreed to do so and said he'd book a dinner for them at a nice restaurant the next night. He, of course, failed to do so and Liz broke up with him. Then the unthinkable happened ... the zombie apocalypse.

Shaun and Ed woke up hung over after a night of excessive boozing due to the recent breakup, at the end of which Shaun wrote a note to himself: "Go round Mum's. Get Liz back. Sort life out." Ed spent most of the night trying to cheer Shaun up, and even did an impression of the chimp Clyde from the Clint Eastwood film *Every Which Way but Loose*. Shaun even passed several zombies as he went down to the store to pick up a soda and ice cream. When he got back, Ed explained that a girl was standing in their backyard. They went out to investigate and at first thought she was drunk. But when she attacked Shaun and they saw a very large man with part of his faced ripped off come from around the corner, they realized they should go back inside.

Only then did Shaun and Ed realize what most of the world already knew. They flipped on the television and learned that the dead were returning to life and attacking the living. As the television anchor told viewers to make sure that all doors were locked, Shaun and Ed looked at one another and realized that they'd left the front door wide open. They turned to see a zombified young man in a tuxedo, with an arm missing, shambling into their living room. They immediately panicked and begin throwing random objects at the one-armed zombie—pillows, game controllers, paper plates, and more. Ed finally picked up a large glass ash tray and smashed the zombie's head in. Ed insisted that they kill the zombies in the backyard. Shaun agreed to this with some coaxing. After a number of repeated failures to kill the zombies via various projectiles such as kitchenware and even old vinyl records (thank goodness the living dead are so slow), Shaun went into the shed and they emerged with a shovel and a cricket bat. They beat down the two zombies and went back inside, where Ed repeated a frequent line in the film by telling Shaun, "You've got red on you."

Brains!

The sci-fi video game that Shaun and Ed are playing at both the beginning and end of the film *Shaun of the Dead* is actually a very real video game called *TimeSplitters 2*.

Only then did Shaun realize that he had forgotten about his Mother's Day date with his mum, as well as the fact that he needed to save Liz. He spoke to his mother on the phone and learned that his overbearing stepfather, Phillip (Bill Nighy), had been bitten. He and Ed set about hatching a plot to save his mum and Liz, and taking everyone to the Winchester pub, where they planned to wait until the whole thing "blows over."

Nothing in Shaun's plan went right. Phillip died. They managed to reach the Winchester, but Shaun's mother was bitten and Shaun was forced to shoot her. Liz's flatmate's boyfriend was torn to pieces. Her flatmate had tried to rescue him, swinging her boyfriend's severed limbs as a weapon as she disappeared into the zombie horde outside, presumably to her death (the film's DVD extras explain that she did survive). Ed was also bitten ... by the same flatmate who had constantly called him a loser. With his group mates dropping like flies and an ever-growing undead horde right outside, Shaun, Liz, and Ed had to battle to stay alive against impossible odds.

City of Rott

City of Rott is one of the lesser-known films of the zombie cinema canon. Released in 2006, this independent animated zombie film was created by Frank Sudol.

City of Rott follows the adventures of a rather crabby elderly man named Fred, who managed to survive a recent zombie outbreak caused by an organism (called a Worm Rott) that had contaminated the water supply. Using only his trusty walker as a weapon, Fred complained and whined his way through the apocalyptic landscape as he ventured out to find himself a new pair of shoes. After all, his feet were killing him ... and what did a few hundred undead matter when comfort was on the line? When faced with the undead, Fred turned into a geriatric killing machine! He used his walker to thrash the walking dead into submission, often in a rather comical yet gruesome fashion.

As Fred continued his quest for new shoes, he kept coming across other survivors. While the crabby old guy would far rather be left alone, apocalypse or not, he soon found himself leading the only group of survivors out of the infected city. With his trusty walker cutting a bloody path before them, could the survivors make it out of the city alive?

Dance of the Dead

The independent zombie horror-comedy *Dance of the Dead* was first shown on October 13, 2008, to audiences at Mann's Chinese Theater.

Brains!

Aside from Mann's Chinese Theater, *Dance of the Dead* was also shown at the 2008 Atlanta Film Festival and the 2008 South by Southwest Film Festival.

Oddly enough, it was released on DVD the following day. The film was directed by Gregg Bishop, with a screenplay written by Joe Ballarini. While this film has not received a large amount of notoriety, it has become a staple of the zombie cinema canon, especially among hardcore fans of the genre.

Dance of the Dead deals with the struggles of a band of high school out-casts in Georgia, who suddenly found themselves battling to save their classmates in the face of a zombie outbreak. The local graveyard, which was located next to a power plant, suddenly became the site of multiple reanimations. Young couples who stopped at the "makeout point," which was located near the graveyard, were the first to be attacked.

Since everyone was at the prom, few notice the growing zombie horde as it advanced toward the local high school. Everyone, that is, but those who did not attend. But who didn't go to the prom? In a word ... misfits. The responsibility of stopping the undead and saving the other kids at the prom now fell into the hands of an unlikely group made up of the school psycho, Kyle; the class clown, Jimmy; and all the members of the school's Science Fiction Club—Jules, Rod, Stephen, and George. They were aided by the local gravedigger, who had been aware of the steadily growing occurrence of reanimations for quite some time (he also taught the kids how to kill them). They were given weapons and eventually led by the school's extremely paranoid, but well armed, gym coach. Adding members of a local punk band, who refused to go to prom after being told they could not play, the group set out to save their classmates and bring an end to the zombie outbreak. Would they survive this *Dance of the Dead?*

Zombieland

Zombieland is one of the most recent, and most successful, zombie films to be released. The film was released in October 2009 and had the second-highest-grossing start for any zombie film (the first being the remake of Romero's *Dawn of the Dead*).

The film follows Columbus and Tallahassee, a pair of survivors of the zombie apocalypse, which was apparently caused by a strain of mad cow disease. Columbus was an anal-retentive, somewhat obsessive-compulsive college student from Austin, Texas. He was trying to reach his parents in Columbus, Ohio, in the hopes that they were still alive. His rather obsessive nature has allowed him to survive, and throughout the film the audience is let in on at least 10 of his 32 "rules" for surviving a zombie apocalypse:

> Rule #1: Cardio
>
> Rule #2: Double-tap (meaning shoot every zombie twice, just to be sure)

Rule #3: Beware of bathrooms

Rule #4: Seatbelts

Rule #7: Travel light

Rule #17: Don't be a hero

Rule #18: Limber up

Rule #22: When in doubt, know your way out

Rule #31: Check the back seat

Rule #32: Enjoy the little things

Columbus eventually encountered the kill-happy cowboy Tallahassee (played by Woody Harrelson), who decided that the zombie apocalypse was what he was born to live through. He was Columbus's polar opposite, wild and reckless. For example, among his plans for the apocalypse was finding the last Twinkies on Earth. He stopped at every store along the way in this search for the soon-to-be-rare pastries.

Brains!

You might notice that all the characters in the film are named after American cities. A coincidence?

As they drove the zombie wasteland together, Columbus and Tallahassee came across a pair of sisters, Wichita (Emma Stone) and her younger sister, Little Rock (Abigail Breslin, best known for her role in *Little Miss Sunshine*). The sisters stole their truck and all their weapons. By a stroke of luck, however, the men found an H2 Hummer full of weapons and tracked down the girls. Unfortunately, the girls succeeded in hijacking the two men yet again. This time, however, the ever-congenial Columbus convinced everyone that it was in their best interest to work together.

As they traveled, Columbus learned from Wichita that the city of Columbus, Ohio, had been lost to the undead. He then had to abandon all hope of finding his parents alive. Having developed feelings for the rather attractive Wichita, he decided to stay with the group. The group learned of a place called Pacific Playland that was rumored to be "zombie free." Along the way, they stopped and spent the night at Bill Murray's mansion estate. Believe it or not, they found Murray alive. He wore zombie makeup and pretended to be undead in order to live among the infected without detection. However, Murray snuck up behind Columbus while he was watching *Ghostbusters*. Thinking he was a zombie, Columbus blew Murray's head off.

After a hasty funeral for the now truly dead Bill Murray, the group continued on for the possible safety of Pacific Playland. Would they make it there alive? And if so, would it really be free of zombies?

The Least You Need to Know

- ◆ *Resident Evil* was the first zombie film to be made in nearly a decade, and it reshaped the entire genre with sci-fi elements.

- ◆ *28 Days Later* technically isn't a zombie film, but it's still considered by many a part of the zombie cinema canon.

- ◆ *Shaun of the Dead* is both a comedy and a tribute to legendary zombie film director George A. Romero.

- ◆ *Zombieland* is technically not a zombie film, since the infected are not actually dead, but insane, flesh-eating people who are infected with a mutated strain of mad cow disease.

Chapter **12**

When Zombie Movies Go Rotten

In This Chapter

- ◆ The use of "Living Dead" in films not affiliated with the Romero film
- ◆ The campiness of the 1985 horror-comedy *Return of the Living Dead*
- ◆ Zombies and … strippers?
- ◆ Unsuccessful Romero remakes

Not all zombie movies are cinematic gems. In fact, many of them are downright awful. Whether by terribly ill-conceived plotlines, untalented filmmaking, atrocious acting, insufficient budgets, or any combination of these, sometimes zombie movies just go rotten. However, even these decaying apples have a place in the realm of zombie fandom—though often as little more than examples of what *not* to do when making a zombie film. What follows is a sampling of works that are generally considered some of the worst zombie films ever made (although certainly there are others that have been overlooked).

The "Living Dead" Rip-Offs

A number of second-rate zombie B-movies have been made on the coattails of George A. Romero's success (for more on Romero, see Chapter 10). Since he has never owned the words "Living Dead," they were up for grabs to anyone who wanted to use them. Sadly, many took advantage of this and made terrible films with the words "Living Dead" in the title. Probably the most well known among these is the campy and poorly put together *Return of the Living Dead.*

Many fans of Romero's *Night of the Living Dead* went to the theaters, only to be disappointed. The movie has nothing to do with any of Romero's films, aside from the fact that they used "Living Dead" in the title. While some still consider the movie a cult classic, many diehard zombie fans take issues with the film.

Issues with the "Returning Dead"

Return of the Living Dead was first released to the public in 1985 as somewhat of a horror-comedy. The story begins with an older man named Frank, who was a worker at a local medical supply warehouse, training the new, younger employee, Freddy. While trying to scare Freddy, Frank took the young man downstairs to the warehouse basement and showed him a canister full of what he claimed was a chemical weapon stored by the army to bring the dead to life. According to Frank, the canister had fallen off the back of a military truck during a brief but contained zombie outbreak. Bet you can guess what happened next. That's right.

The seal on the container broke, causing both Frank and Freddy to inhale its contents. The virus spread through the warehouse, reviving a cadaver in the freezer. The cadaver began screaming, and they let it out. Frank told Freddy that all they had to do was hit it on the head. So they put the business end of a pickaxe through its skull. Nothing happened. The zombie just kept on screaming. From here on out, things only got worse ... and weirder.

Most zombie fans have two main issues with these films. Number one, this was the first movie to depict zombies eating the brains of the living. This makes no sense, since without a brain, the whole idea of reanimation becomes a little hard to swallow. Second, zombie fans did not like the idea that the "Return" zombies could not be killed with a blow to the brain ... because they didn't have brains to begin with. This whole "brainlessness" factor is further compounded by the fact that the zombies could talk. Speech requires thought ... which requires a brain. The whole zombie concept of *Return of the Living Dead* has just never sat well with many zombie fans, though most would agree that any discussion of zombie films would require its mention. After all, even this book has been influenced by the "brains inclusion" of these films, as evident from the *Brains!* sidebars.

Zombie Strippers

The rather odd B-movie *Zombie Strippers* was released by Sony Pictures in 2008. Believe it or not, the movie is based on a French play called *Rhinoceros,* by Eugene Ionesco. The cast of the film is a collection of oddities, and the film stars porn star Jenna Jameson, horror legend Robert Englund (best known for his role as Freddie Krueger), and mixed-martial-arts competitor Tito Ortiz. Jammed full of cheesy lines, bad acting, and loads of absurdity, *Zombie Strippers* most certainly deserves a special place in history as one of the most terrible zombie movies of all time.

The movie takes place in a hypothetical near future. George W. Bush was elected to his fourth term and dissolved the U.S. Congress. The country was embroiled in so many wars it is unfathomable, and Bush took up arms against just about everyone—in addition to Afghanistan and Iraq, also fighting Alaska (which seceded from the union), Canada, France, Iran, Syria, and Venezuela. The country did not have enough soldiers to effectively fight the many wars Bush had started. To make matters worse for the story's protagonists, nudity had been outlawed.

In a secret government laboratory in Sartre, Nebraska, a seriously stereotypical "mad scientist" named Dr. Chushfeld (played by Brad Milne) succeeded in developing a serum that could reanimate the bodies of dead soldiers so they could be sent back into battle. When the virus escaped (of course), a special team of Marines, the "Z Squad," was sent in to mop up the situation. One member of the unit, Byrdflough (that's right, as in "Bird Flu," played by Zak Kilberg), was bitten and ran off to avoid being exterminated. He eventually collapsed in an alley behind a strip club called the Rhino (bet you can see where this is going). He died, reanimated, and went into the strip club ... typical zombie Marine.

Ian Essko (played by Englund) was the owner/operator of the Rhino and recently hired a new girl named Jesse (played by Jennifer Holland). Jesse was stripping to raise money her grandmother needed for an operation. She soon met the Nietzsche-reading, ultra-intelligent Kat (played by Jenna Jameson), the club's star dancer. Kat went out to start her routine but was infected when the zombified Marine Byrdflough jumped on stage and attacked her. Kat then turned into a zombie. The weird thing is, this only seemed to increase her popularity as a stripper (which, you have to admit, seems just a little creepy).

The other strippers started losing customers to the zombified Kat. In fact, all the male patrons soon preferred zombie strippers over living ones. One at a time, the strippers began voluntarily allowing themselves to be turned into zombies to avoid losing anymore paying customers to the zombified strippers—well, except for the vampire-goth stripper named Lilith (played by rock musician Roxy Saint), who just thought that becoming one of the living dead would be cool.

Essko kept things under control and kept the money pouring in by keeping the zombie strippers in a cage in the cellar. Of course, they eventually escaped and started running rampant through the club. The living strippers then had to fight to survive against the living dead strippers.

When all seemed lost, the "Z Squad" showed up, having tracked Byrdflough to the location. As they proceeded to mop up, they were halted when new orders came in. As it turned out, President Bush had issued orders that the zombies be allowed to escape. The Bush administration hoped that a zombie virus outbreak would be enough to distract the American people from how terrible Bush's leadership was, that he was completely mishandling the wars (all of them) and that the economy was worse than ever. So in the end, nothing was really resolved, dealt with, or addressed ... unless you count their commentary on former-President Bush's lack of leadership skills.

Zombies! Zombies! Zombies!

Another stripper-related, B-rate zombie film is known in the United States (barely) under the title *Zombies! Zombies! Zombies!* In Japan and Europe, however, it was released under the somewhat more provocative (or just less misleading) title *Strippers vs. Zombies.* This slice of straight-to-video horror-comedy was released in 2008 and directed by Jason Murphy.

The plot of the film is basically that a scientist searching for the cure to cancer ended up making a serum that accelerates cell growth. A local drug addict came in to steal dope but mistook a vile of the serum for drugs. The druggie shared the "dope" with a group of friendly hookers. Apparently, the serum did more than just accelerate cell growth—it turned all of them into zombies. The now-zombified prostitutes' pimp was soon running for his life and took refuge in a nearby strip club called the Grindhouse. The strippers and the pimp then had to defend the club against the increasing horde of zombies descending upon them. It's a formula for stereotypically bad filmmaking.

Day of the Dead (Remake)

This *Day of the Dead* was marketed as a remake of the original George A. Romero film, but it didn't deliver on that promise since its final form did not at all resemble Romero's classic. Directed by Steve Miner (who directed *Friday the 13th II* and *III*) and written by Jeffrey Reddick, the original plan was for the film to be released nationwide. Instead, it ended up as just another poorly made raping of a Romero classic and was given nothing more than straight-to-video distribution.

Though the movie is supposed to be set in the town of Leadville, California, it was shot in Bulgaria, which is fairly obvious when you watch the film. The film begins with a group of teens having a make-out party in an abandoned building—including the film's main protagonists, Nina and Bud. On their way back home to Leadville, they came upon a military roadblock and learned that some kind of disaster had happened in the city. A man soon approached from the other side and begged for medical attention for his sick child.

The teens met Captain Rhodes (played by Ving Rhames), Corporal Cross (Mena Suvari), Private Cryinside (Stark Sands), and Private Salazar (Nick Cannon). Two of the teens, Nina and Bud, were taken past the blockade by Corporal Cross to see Nina's mother (who had fallen ill). Bud found that her mother was sick but was able to retrieve her brother, Trevor. They then went to the house of Kyle, a friend of her brother's, and found both of his parents' mutilated, gnawed-upon corpses hidden behind a curtain. They were all soon taken to a nearby hospital. While there, they didn't realize that all the "wounded" were actually infected with a zombie virus.

While the wounded awaited treatment, they suddenly went stiff and soon reanimated. The hospital turned into a slaughterhouse. The group was soon back where the film started, at the abandoned building.

Basically, by now you should be noticing something—the plot bears absolutely no resemblance to Romero's *Day of the Dead*. In fact one might suspect that the creators of this false remake had never even seen the original film, since any human being who had seen it would know that the plot of the new film is completely unrelated. Sadly, this is yet another film that tried to piggyback to success on the legendary name of George A. Romero. By itself, the movie could at least be digested. But the fact that it claims to be a remake of a Romero classic but fails to include any of the same settings or characters from it, has landed this film in some very hot water with Romero admirers and zombie cinema fans in general. For more on the original Romero classic *Day of the Dead*, see Chapter 10.

Zombi: The Italian Romero Rip-Off

George A. Romero's *Dawn of the Dead* was released in Europe under the title of *Zombi*. In 1979, director Lucio Fulci hoped to use the success of Romero films to give his waning career a boost. So he took a zombie movie that he'd actually made *before* the release of *Dawn of the Dead* and marketed it as a direct sequel to the Romero film by giving it the title *Zombi 2*. Well, Fulci certainly succeeded. *Zombi 2* turned out to be his most successful film and made him a horror icon in Europe.

Brains!

Zombi 2 was markedly more violent than Romero's films. In fact, it was so violent that it came under fire from many censorship groups and even British Parliament, the majority of which was ultra-conservative at the time. In fact, it was banned in the United Kingdom until the late 1990s.

The movie starts with a yacht drifting in New York Harbor. As a squad from the Harbor Patrol boarded the yacht to investigate, they were attacked by the very intimidating, and very zombified, Captain Haggerty (captain of the vessel). Haggerty bit out the neck of one of the patrolman. Another patrolman, named Bill, opened fire and knocked the zombie sea captain into the water.

Brains!

In recent years, many of the more notoriously ridiculous or cheesy scenes from *Zombi 2* have become viral videos on YouTube. One most notable scene is of Captain Haggerty battling and biting into a tiger shark (believe it or not, they used a *real* shark up until the bite scenes) while submerged in the ocean. The name of Canadian rock band *Fake Shark– Real Zombie* was taken from this scene.

When police investigated the origins of the yacht, they discovered that it was owned by a man named Bowles (played by Ugo Bologna). They called in his daughter, Anne Bowles (played by Tisa Farrow), for questioning when they failed to locate the man. Anne explained that her father had recently left on a research trip to a tropical island. It wasn't long before the press found out about the "mystery boat," and journalist Peter West (played by British actor Ian McCulloch) was assigned to the story.

While Peter was investigating the boat, he crossed paths with Anne. They discovered a note left behind by her father in which he explained that he was on the island of Matool and had been stricken by some mysterious illness. Anne and Peter agreed to work together to find him, and immediately searched out a sea captain who knew the way to the island. They found a captain named Brian Hull (played by Pier Luigi Conti).

Believe it or not, Ian McCulloch, the male lead actor in *Zombi 2*, never saw the full version of the film when it was released in Europe. Back in his native United Kingdom, the film was banned. Not until the "uncut" (meaning, "insanely gory") version of *Zombi 2* was released on laser disc in 1998 did McCulloch see the entire film for the first time. He is said to have been appalled at how bloody and gory the final cut turned out to be. Apparently, he had never seen many of the film's ultra-brutal kill scenes. For example, there is one particularly chilling kill scene in which a woman has her eye gouged out slowly with a piece of splintered wood.

The island of Matool was home to the insane Dr. Menard (played by Richard Johnson), who was trying to uncover the secret behind the island's strange effects on the dead. The dead of the island reanimated and attacked the living. Dr. Menard's anxiety-ridden wife (seriously, it is stressful just to watch her), Paola (played by Olga Karlatos), hated him for bringing them to a cursed place where they were constantly under attack by zombies, and wanted off the island. But Menard refused to leave, claiming that his research was too important to abandon.

When Peter, Anne, and Brian arrived on Matool, they were greeted by a welcome party of ferocious undead. This sparked a long, violent, gore-filled, blood-spattered chain of events that eventually ended with most of the characters dying terrible, painful deaths. Dr. Menard … dead. Mrs. Menard … also dead. Brian got infected with the zombie virus and also kicked the bucket. In fact, Peter and Anne were the only ones who made it back to the boat—well, alive, anyway. They tied up the now-zombified Brian, planning to take him back to civilization as evidence that their story was real.

As they ventured out into the ocean, they believed that their ordeal was over. However, the boat's radio soon crackled to life. Listening to the transmissions, they learned that the nightmare they'd just survived was only the beginning. The living dead were overrunning New York City. Apparently, the cop killed by Haggerty had reanimated and the zombified Captain Haggerty had found his way out of the harbor. The two had spawned an army of zombies that were eating everyone in the city. The movie rather abruptly ends here.

Night of the Living Dead 3D

Night of the Living Dead 3D is currently on the fast-track to being officially dubbed the worst zombie movie of all time. It is already widely considered the worst remake of a George A. Romero film in the history of zombie cinema.

Brains!

Don't confuse the horrible *Night of the Living Dead 3D* with the 1990 Tom Savini remake of *Night of the Living Dead*. Savini's film (which was based on a revised screenplay by George A. Romero) is fairly good and true to the original, whereas the "3D" remake is an atrocity (and was certainly *not* endorsed by Romero).

The only reason this movie was even allowed to be made is that no one owns the rights to the original *Night of the Living Dead.* Therefore, any film hack with a desire to do so can attempt to remake the film. While widely anticipated during its initial production, fan opinions soon turned south as more details (few of them good) began to be learned about *3D.* First of all, they did not ask for permission from Romero to make the film (which many who remake his films tend to do as a show of respect), even though they had scenes from the original film playing on the television in many scenes of the *3D* remake. Any Romero remake made without at least getting a nod from the man has met with catastrophic failure.

Though originally planned for theatrical release, the film got shoved into straight-to-video distribution. The DVDs went on sale in October 2007, with both a 3D version (equipped with four pairs of old-school 3D glasses) and a normal 2D version.

The reception of the film is pretty consistent across the board. The general opinion of the film is that it is a poorly made rip-off that was created to make a profit off the 40-year anniversary of Romero's debut film *Night of the Living Dead.* There was even an "Anniversary Edition" of the DVD title released, to maximize salability.

The Least You Need to Know

◆ Many attempts to make remakes of Romero films have met with epic failure, usually because they were made without his consultation or consent.

◆ Many films have tried to ride on the coattails of Romero's success by using titles that give the false impression that they are approved sequels to his works.

◆ The only remake of *Night of the Living Dead* that received Romero's blessing was the 1990 Tom Savini film.

Chapter 13

The Rise of the Video Game Zombie

In This Chapter

◆ *Resident Evil*'s revival of the viral zombie in pop culture

◆ Zombie-themed survival-horror games such as *Dead Rising* and *Left 4 Dead*

◆ The heavily revised 1990s gaming classic *Zombies Ate My Neighbors*

◆ The vehicular mayhem of the zombie-themed PC driving game *Zombie Driver*

Video games have been allowing everyday Joes to unleash a rain of digital fury on an array of baddies—robots, aliens, giant gorillas, evil turtles, and, of course, zombies. Ever since the debut of *Resident Evil* in 1996, the zombie video game has exploded into a multigenre gaming theme. Zombies are the most popular and common theme of the first-person shooters and survival-horror video games of today. Wanna beat a zombie to death? There's a game for that. Wanna shoot a zombie in the face at point-blank range? There's a game for that, too. Or maybe you've always dreamed of driving your car through an undead legion, cutting a bloody path that leaves nothing but mayhem in your wake? Well, you are in luck, my friend … there's a game for that as well.

Resident Evil

When you mention the great zombie video games of the past, one of the first titles that inevitably comes up is *Resident Evil*. Known in Japan by the title *Biohazard*, this game introduced a whole new generation of fans to the idea of flesh-eating zombies. Most of the kids who were too young for the zombie films of the late '80s and early '90s had grown up playing games like the infamous *Doom*. The eerie mood of the original *Resident Evil* game affected gamers like nothing before.

Resident Evil first appeared in 1996 on the Sony PlayStation. It quickly became the most successful video game of its time. Two years later, it was followed by a sequel, *Resident Evil 2*, and a third edition of the game came out a year after that. Since then, *Resident Evil* has spawned myriad sequels, offshoots, and side-plot games on a number of different gaming systems, from Sony to Sega to Nintendo. Eventually, the creator of the game, Shinji Mikami, made it exclusively available on Nintendo game systems. Capcom made a few side games for other systems, despite this, by manipulating the loophole that these were not directly tied to the original plotline.

You play the game as a member of the elite S.T.A.R.S. (Special Tactics and Rescue Service) Alpha Team, a near-paramilitary unit of the Raccoon City Police Department. When your team comes to investigate the recently downed helicopter of the S.T.A.R.S. Bravo Team, the only thing found is a gnawed-off hand. The team is attacked by dogs, and the chopper pilot leaves Alpha Team high and dry. The stranded team is forced to take refuge in a nearby mansion, with the jaws of infected dogs right on their heels. But the nightmare is only beginning. Alpha Team consists of the following characters, many of which the player controls at different stages of the game:

- ◆ Albert Wesker

- ◆ Chris Redfield

- Barry Burton

- Jill Valentine

Shortly after barricading themselves in the mansion, the team hears a gunshot that seems to come from somewhere in the house. This is where the player is first given control of a character (Jill Valentine).

Anyone who is old enough (or young enough) to have played the original version of *Resident Evil* remembers this scene, which introduces the player to the zombies of the game. Your character comes up behind a man who is hunched over on his knees. You move forward to investigate. You can hear strange sounds, as if he is chewing or tearing something. As the player, you already anticipate what is coming and brace for a shock. The man stops moving, as if he has heard you, and turns his head your direction. As he does, there is a crunch. A half-eaten severed head tumbles to the ground before you. It is the head of Kenneth Sullivan, a member of the MIA Bravo Team. Then you see the man's face—stark white, with blank eyes and a blood-stained mouth. Needless to say, this scene scared many gamers in its day.

After this, things just get increasingly difficult and odd for the player. It soon becomes clear that this is no ordinary mansion, as it is equipped with an unusual amount of high-tech surveillance, traps, and lethal security measures. As the game goes on, the player finds fragment documents that eventually explain at least part of what's happening. The mansion is actually the cover for a secret research facility that lies beneath it. This facility was working with a substance dubbed the "T-Virus," which recently escaped the clean zone and has now infected everything in the house and surrounding areas. The T-Virus infects, mutates, and reanimates anything it touches—humans, animals, insects, even birds—turning them into vicious killing machines.

The events of the game and the ending change, depending on what decisions the player makes. Most of the endings, however, are not exactly happy ones. For example, one requires you to kill one teammate in order to save yourself and another. If you sacrifice your teammate, you save the other one and both of you escape Raccoon City. If you don't kill the teammate, you and everyone else die at the end.

Dead Rising

The game *Dead Rising* was produced in Japan by Keiji Inafune and developed by gaming giant Capcom for the Xbox 360 game console. The game was first released in Japan in September 2006 and in the United States in August 2006. It was hailed as one of the best survival-horror *RPGs* ever. In February 2009, a new version of the game was created for the interactive Wii console, under the title *Dead Rising: Chop 'Til You Drop.* A sequel to the game, *Dead Rising 2*, is currently in development and planned for release sometime in 2010.

Moooooaaaaan...

> RPG stands for role-playing game, a genre of game in which the player assumes the role of a character. In RPG games, playable characters are usually customizable and become stronger or "level up" as more battles are fought.

Dead Rising follows the adventures of Frank West (the character controlled by the player), a journalist who finds himself trapped inside a shopping mall in the middle of a zombie outbreak. Frank has come to the fictional town of Willamette, Colorado, to investigate reports that the town has been sealed off by the National Guard. He has himself dropped via helicopter onto the roof of the town mall. Before heading inside, Frank instructs the pilot to return for him in 72 hours. When he gets inside, however, Frank realizes that perhaps he should have scheduled an earlier pickup.

When he gets inside, he sees that the front entrance of the mall is covered with zombies trying to get in. A panic-stricken woman who is looking for her lost dog unlocks the doors, and the zombies flood inside. The survivors are ordered to make a mad dash for the mall's security office by a Homeland Security officer named Brad. Unfortunately, Brad and Frank are the only ones to make it there alive. The mall janitor, Otis, is already in the office and welds the door shut once Brad and Frank are inside. With him is another Homeland Security officer named Jessie.

The mall is now wall-to-wall zombies, and Frank must find a way out of this deathtrap. And zombies aren't the only problem. It appears that the virus doesn't kill and reanimate everyone. Some people are simply driven to homicidal madness by the infection. Brad and Jessie, who seem to know more than they are letting on, explain that these infected persons are referred to as Psychopaths. Throughout the game, Frank and Brad also have encounters with a mysterious and violent character named Carlito. They are also joined in the security room by a man named Dr. Barnaby and a woman named Isabella. When Barnaby turns out to be infected and goes psychotic, it is learned that he headed a secret research lab in Central America where he developed a species of wasp that could transform people into zombies. It is also learned that Isabella is the sister of Carlito, who were once residents of the village of Santa Cabeza where Dr. Barnaby had carried out his experiments.

Don't Get Bit!

> Santa Cabeza, like Willamette, Colorado, is not a real location, and the name of the village is probably meant as a joke. The Spanish title of Santa Cabeza, roughly translated in English, means something like "Saint Head/Skull/Brain." This would make sense, since zombies can be killed only with a fatal shot to the head.

Apparently, a queen wasp escaped from the research facility and infected the entire population of Santa Cabeza. The United States sent in a special forces team to exterminate the queen and everyone infected, covering it up in the press as a raid on a drug cartel. Carlito became enraged by the slaughter of his friends, family, and neighbors. He found some surviving wasps and brought them to Willamette to exact his revenge upon Dr. Barnaby. The evil doctor completes his transformation into a zombie, and Brad puts a bullet through his brainpan.

But Willamette is not the end of Carlito's revenge. Beneath the mall, he has set up five large explosives that are covered with millions of immature wasp larvae. When they blow up, they will expel the larvae into the atmosphere and cause a worldwide pandemic of zombies. Frank goes after the bombs as Brad chases after Carlito. Luckily, Frank (as the player) succeeds in disarming the bombs. Brad, however, is infected while trying to capture Carlito.

Frank and the others now realize that they must find some way to escape. Isabella explains that her brother keeps his laptop and a jamming device (which is preventing anyone from calling for help) in a secret hideout in the mall. Using the security cameras, Homeland Security officer Jessie tracks Carlito to an underground meat-packing facility. Unfortunately, he is immediately captured by a Psychopath butcher. Frank rescues Jessie, and together they take down Carlito. They fail to obtain the password to his laptop before Carlito succumbs to his many wounds. In his dying moments, Carlito asks them to give his locket to Isabella. She uses the locket to figure out how to open the laptop and shuts down the jamming device.

Jessie sends out a distress call to Homeland Security. However, she is told that the U.S. government has sent out yet another "cleanup crew." A special forces unit soon arrives and starts killing anyone in sight, infected or not. From here, any sequence of ending events might occur. One interesting element of *Dead Rising* is that it has a flexible plotline. Even more than in its predecessor, *Resident Evil*, there are multiple ways in which the game can end. How the final events of the game pan out, and how it ultimately ends, depends on the decisions of the player (past and present).

Zombies Ate My Neighbors

Zombies Ate My Neighbors was developed by LucasArts in 1993 and released by Konami for the Sega Genesis, and was meant to be a tribute to the horror classics of the 1950s and '60s. It was a precursor to the first-person shooter games of modern times, a part of the so-called "run and gun" genre in which players controlled a character that ran across a two-dimensional landscape (usually seen from an above view) while killing enemies. Despite some who opposed the game, it was a commercial success. However, the sequel, released in 1994 under the title *Ghoul Patrol*, did not fare so well.

Brains!

Zombies Ate My Neighbors was released before the creation of the ESRB, which now gives specific ratings to video games. As a result, it was subjected to censorship. At the time, Nintendo of America even ordered that all depictions of gore and red blood be either removed from games completely or at least replaced with green "ooze."

Zombies Ate My Neighbors allows the player to choose between one of two characters, the teenaged Zeke or Julie. In two-player mode, both characters can be played. The players must then fight their way through the map of suburbs, strange pyramids, malls, and more. They must face a horde of enemies, consisting of the usual stereotypical movie monsters such as vampires, werewolves, and demonic dolls. And, of course, there are the zombies to deal with.

The game has 48 levels, as well as 6 bonus levels. The goal of the game is to rescue your neighbors. Every level has a neighbor in need of rescue, and successfully saving the neighbors will open up a portal to the next level. At least one neighbor must be rescued in order for the player to advance to the next level. However, if all of the potential 10 neighbors on a level are killed, then it is game over. The same thing happens if the player runs out of lives. Extra lives can be gained by saving all the neighbors on any level.

Left 4 Dead

Left 4 Dead is a *cooperative first-person shooter*, and one of the most popular survival-horror video games in recent history. The game was initially being developed by Turtle Rock Games but was purchased halfway through its production by the Valve Corporation, which adapted the game to their exclusive Source 3D gaming engine. *Left 4 Dead* was released in November 2008 and is available on Windows PCs and Xbox 360.

Mooooooaaaaan...

A **cooperative first-person shooter** is a fairly new game type that allows multiple players to work together in a gaming environment. *Left 4 Dead* works with four-person teams, and in the absence of live players, the remaining playable characters are controlled by the Valve Corporation's Source engine's artificial intelligence (AI).

Left 4 Dead is set in a world gone mad, and players begin their journeys in the wake of a zombie virus pandemic as one of the game's four characters. Players may begin in any of four game modes:

   ◆ **Single-player:** The other allied characters are controlled by the game engine's AI.

◆ **AI-player combo:** There is more than one live player, but one or more of the four characters is controlled by the AI.

◆ **Co-op/four-player:** All characters are controlled by live players.

◆ **Versus:** Your four-player team will be pitted against another team, mainly in online play.

◆ **Survival:** Also a four-player co-op mode (but can be done with AI as well), this is more about how long the team can survive.

Bralns!

Left 4 Dead has received a number of awards and distinctions from such prestigious organizations as the Academy of Interactive Arts and Sciences and the British Academy of Film and Television Arts.

In the game, players encounter more than just the stereotypical zombie. In fact, the game has a number of different zombie types that players must contend with, each with its own set of nasty abilities:

◆ **Undead:** A regular, run-of-the-mill zombie, though the zombies in this game are of the "fast" variety (meaning they can run).

◆ **Boomer:** Bloated zombies that resemble a fat guy, these run at you and explode, releasing a flood of toxic vomit and bile that temporarily blinds any player in its range.

◆ **Hunter:** An agile zombie type that pounces on players, often from a concealed/elevated position, and tears them apart.

◆ **Smoker:** A zombie equipped with a long barbed tongue that it uses to snatch players from a distance, often before the other members realize what has happened.

◆ **Tank:** A big, hulking figure, like a zombie on steroids, this type is very strong and even more durable. Tanks slam players through walls, crush vehicles, and hurl debris. It often takes every bit of firepower a team has to bring them down.

◆ **Witch:** This is a creepy zombie type, making a sound that resembles a crying child. Leave them alone, and you are fine. Get too close or make too much noise, and they'll attack. They can incapacitate and kill players relatively quickly.

Brains!

> One piece of advice while playing *Left 4 Dead:* never, ever, ever shoot a parked vehicle. The game's zombies are attracted to high-pitched sounds, and shooting a car can set off a car alarm, which immediately brings a hellstorm of undead down on your head, as any zombie in earshot will immediately swarm to your position. Don't believe it? Try it yourself and find out.

Both *Left 4 Dead* and its November 2009 sequel, *Left 4 Dead 2*, follow a similar plotline. Both games follow the journey of four survivors during a zombie apocalypse. Players must fight their way from one safehouse to another as they try to make their way out of the chaos. The sequel, however, has been set in the southern United States. The new cast of four players must fight their way from Savannah, Georgia, to New Orleans, Louisiana.

Brains!

> Much like the hit movie *Zombieland, Left 4 Dead 2* includes a mission in which players must battle the undead in an abandoned carnival.

Zombie Driver (PC Game)

Released in November 2009 by EXOR Studios, the PC-only game *Zombie Driver* delivers some serious blood spatter to its players. Players must drive through a zombie-infested landscape, all while trying to save the few remaining survivors of the outbreak. The game is fueled by the Ogre3D gaming engine and the PhysX, of the NVIDIA corporation.

Unlike nearly every other zombie-themed game ever developed, *Zombie Driver* is not a shooter game. While it might classify as a survival-horror game, the player's main weapon is a vehicle—that's right, you hit the undead with your car. This game replaces the violent shooter with a race-against-time plotline, in which the player must run down the hordes of zombies, and just about any other obstacle in the way, with a car. As more zombies are killed and more survivors rescued, the player receives more resources with which to upgrade his or her zombie-killing vehicle. Or the player can simply buy a new vehicle altogether.

The Least You Need to Know

- *Resident Evil* was one of the first zombie-themed 3D games and gave birth to the survival-horror gaming genre.

- *Dead Rising,* known to Wii players as *Chop 'Til You Drop,* is one of the most successful survival-horror RPGs in history.

- *Zombies Ate My Neighbors* was originally developed by LucasArts as a tribute to the horror films of the 1950s and '60s.

- *Left 4 Dead* and its sequel, *Left 4 Dead 2,* both follow a team of four characters in a battle to survive a zombie apocalypse.

- *Left 4 Dead* requires players to contend with multiple zombie types.

- *Zombie Driver* is a new zombie-themed game that replaces the usual shooter by allowing players to use their vehicles as a primary weapon.

Part 4

Zombies and Us

Throughout this book, I argue that zombies are often a metaphorical reflection for all that is ignoble and detestable about humankind. However, the zombie genre has also brought out the best in many people. Zombies are now a large part of our culture. In Part 4, we look at the world of zombie fandom—beginning with the growing subcultures of zombie survivalist groups, zombie walks, and zombie flash mobs. At the end of Part 4, we briefly examine the "what ifs" of the zombie phenomenon. After all, if you're prepared for zombies, then you're prepared for just about anything the world can throw at you.

Chapter 14

Zombie Survivalist Groups

In This Chapter

- ◆ The real-world applications of preparing for a hypothetical zombie apocalypse

- ◆ The increasing presence of the zombie survivalist subculture on social networking sites

- ◆ The organization and skills of the Zombie Coalition Offensive Response Elite

- ◆ The Zombie Squad's dedication to education and community service

- ◆ The elusive purpose of the Jim Rage Elite Zombie Hunting Squad

- ◆ Zombie survivalist web resources, such as the Zombie Survival Wiki

Zombie survivalist groups are quickly establishing themselves as one of the prominent subcultures of the modern world. Hundreds of groups are currently in operation, both in the

United States and throughout the world. Their membership is diverse, and members range from zombie movie fans to survivalist enthusiasts to firearms experts. At first glance, something called a "zombie survivalist" group sounds insane. But upon closer inspection, it's not as crazy an idea as you might first think.

If You're Prepared for Zombies ...

Most uninitiated think a zombie *survivalist* group would be a gathering of delusional individuals who believe that the zombie apocalypse is a very real threat that requires immediate preparation. However, this is not the case. The general motto of most zombie survivalist groups is, "If you're prepared for zombies, you're prepared for anything." And this is certainly true.

Moooooaaaaan...

A **survivalist** is an individual who practices a lifestyle that increases his or her chances of survival in the event of a disaster. Normal ("nonzombie") survivalism often focuses on gathering proper supplies and learning practical skills to facilitate one's survival in real-world situations such as floods, earthquakes, and riots.

Think about it for a moment. Zombies represent the worst possible scenario for human survival, and the same kinds of supplies, skills, and knowledge are required to survive a zombie apocalypse as are required for any other survival situation (such as riots, home-front warfare, and natural disasters). In fact, members of a zombie survivalist group will tell you that they have used their zombie survival supplies and training in real-life disaster situations.

Take, for example, the recent natural disasters of hurricanes Ike and Katrina. Many members of zombie survivalist groups were in the path of these hurricanes. When the hurricanes hit, these zombie survivalists already had the necessary supplies to survive. Meanwhile, their neighbors were struggling to locate such necessities as food, water, electricity generators, and fuel.

Consider this basic list of supplies and skills that most zombie survivalists adhere to (for more on actual zombie survival skills, see Chapter 15):

- 14 to 90 days' worth of nonperishable food

- A personal water source (such as a well for groundwater), and/or 14 to 90 days' worth of drinkable water

- At least one firearm (with which you have practiced extensively), with 1,000 to 10,000 rounds of ammunition

- A gasoline electricity generator with 2 to 4 weeks' worth of fuel

- A sturdy melee/close-combat weapon (again, with which you have practiced extensively), as well as some form of martial arts/ close-combat training

As people fight over necessities during times of disaster, or wait help-lessly to be rescued while suffering from hunger and dehydration, these individuals have plenty of both. When looting begins in certain disaster regions, zombie survivalists are able to fortify their homes with sand-bags and deter looters by brandishing their firearms in a show of force. So, as you can see, being prepared for the hypothetical possibility of zombies certainly does mean that you are prepared for any real survival threat that the world could throw at you.

Zombie Survival on Social Networking Sites

Social networking sites such as Facebook and MySpace have become host to hundreds of zombie survivalist groups. On Facebook alone, for example, a group-search for "zombie survivors" yields roughly 300 individual groups. On MySpace, a search for "zombie" yields a mix of roughly 500 profiles for various individuals and organizations, most of which are related to zombie survival.

Brains!

Social networking sites may be more secure than open chat sites. However, this does not necessarily mean they should be considered 100 percent safe. You should never assume that a person you meet online is telling you the truth, and this rule also applies to these sites' zombie survivalist groups. If the group does not have its own website (one that is not hosted by MySpace or Facebook), then you should ask around and do some checking before concluding that the group is legit.

Social networking sites are often a perfect home for zombie survivalist groups. Memberships to such sites are free and come with convenient features such as messaging, blogging, and wall posts. This means that members can be linked in one virtual location, even if they are in different places geographically. Creating a website for a zombie survivalist group can prove to be a hassle and rarely, if ever, is free. Therefore, perhaps it should not be surprising that more than half of the zombie survivalist groups in the world can be found only on social networking sites.

ZCORE

ZCORE stands for Zombie Coalition Offensive Response Elite. Like many zombie survivalist groups, pinning down specific details about the founders is a bit difficult. Their official website (zcorezombiesurvival. webs.com) offers only the first names of their founders—Tony, Jess, and Brandon. However, they are perhaps one of the most interesting and well-organized zombie survivalist groups one could hope to find.

Membership to the organization is the $4 cost of your membership card. ZCORE currently has active chapters (or ZCORE Teams) in 26 U.S. states—from New York to Texas to California. Team members are organized into a number of task-specific roles, and each must choose and become proficient in one of the 38 ZCORE skill/expertise sets, such as these:

- Close Range Combat Specialist
- Firearm Specialist
- Medic
- Sharpshooter/Marksman
- Survival Expert
- Chef
- Hunting/Fishing Specialist
- Computer Specialist
- Technological Support
- Vehicle Manager/Vehicle Expert

One's role on the team, however, has no bearing on your rank. ZCORE has a very specific rank structure. Promotion from the rank of cadet and up requires the member to successfully complete a rank exam, which is to be evaluated by the team leader(s) (if the team has a higher-ranked member, of course) and then passed on via e-mail to the main organization. Once approved, the member may wear his or her new rank insignia, the specific illustrations of which are available on the website. The rank structure of ZCORE teams, from lowest to highest, is organized as follows:

- Cadet
- Private
- Corporal
- Sergeant
- Master Sergeant
- Lieutenant
- Colonel
- Commander
- Major
- General

Even if one does not choose to join ZCORE, the website offers a variety of free downloads (such as wallpaper) that are pretty cool. And their forum offers any number of interesting conversation topics—for example, hypothetical situations one might encounter during a zombie apocalypse, how the ZCORE "Outbreak Level Chart" is organized, suggested supplies and gear, and even a discussion of zombie cinema.

Zombie Squad

The Zombie Squad credo is, "We make dead things deader." The Zombie Squad's mission statement, as posted on their website (zombiehunters.org), explains their intentions as follows:

> Zombie Squad's mission is to educate the public about the importance of personal preparedness and self-reliance, to increase its

readiness to respond to a number of disasters such as earthquakes, floods, or zombie outbreaks.

The Zombie Squad currently hosts 13 chapters in the United States, as well as 1 in Canada and another in the United Kingdom. Receiving approval for an authorized Zombie Squad chapter is not as simple as in other such organizations and, according to the organization's bylaws, requires the following:

- No less than three active members. (This is the minimum number of officers/administrators required for each chapter, and there is paperwork involved.)

- Each chapter must host a *minimum* of two charity events every year (food drives, blood drives, and so on).

- Chapters are required to hold at least one meeting every other month to plan events.

- Chapter meetings should be open to the public, to encourage recruitment of new members.

What really sets the Zombie Squad apart from other zombie survivalist groups is its high level of dedication to community service. The Zombie Squad members regularly dedicate their time and energy to charitable programs such as Habitat for Humanity. They also frequently hold food drives and fund-raising events for a number of disaster relief organizations, such as the American Red Cross and Direct Relief International. However, they also dedicate efforts to other charities, such as Save the Children, Feed My People, and the American Cancer Society.

While the Zombie Squad certainly goes above and beyond the call of duty when it comes to community service, you will find that this is a frequent element of zombie survivalist groups. Some groups use zombies as a way to mentor kids and young adults about such things as firearms safety and the importance of self-reliance.

In addition to their community service projects, the Zombie Squad offers "Zombie Preparedness Training Seminars." These well-organized and very informative seminars are meant to make survival fun and are used to help fund the Zombie Squad organization's activities.

They have specific training sessions for all walks of life. For example, their available seminars are as follows:

- **Government and Law Enforcement Agencies:** Teaches local and federal law enforcement how to properly respond to a zombie outbreak

- **Civilian businesses:** Teaches offices how to develop response policies for zombie outbreaks

- **Schools and universities:** Teaches how to react when the outbreak comes to the campus

- **Conventions:** A regular sight at zombie and horror conventions, such as the recent Zombie-Con 2009

- **Neighborhood Watch Programs:** How to keep the block secure against the hordes of the undead

Jim Rage's Elite Zombie Hunting Squad

If you ever have the opportunity to ask a member of Jim Rage's Elite Zombie Hunting Squad (JREZHS) the obvious question "Who is Jim Rage?", you will likely receive an answer about a human being so amazing that it almost seems impossible for him to exist. Don't say this to them, though, because to the members of the JREZHS, he is very real. When asked about their founder in an e-mail, one of the group's current leading members, who goes by the name of "Wild West" Winfrey, offered the following explanation for inclusion in this book:

> The founder of our organization, James Gandhi Rage, has been in the business of re-exterminating the undead since the age of 16. In 1986, he formed the Jim Rage Elite Zombie Hunting Squad. In 1988, Jim settled in Blue Springs, Vermont, to have a base of operations. The decision to work out of this area was based on a few things: number 1, the disproportionately large zombie infestation; number 2, the tax incentives; and number 3, the beautiful fall colors.

It was in Blue Springs that Jim recruited a number of hearty young men to form the inner circle of the organization. Jim Rage and his new charges have been battling ever since their founding to rid the world of the undead scourge. Their tales of adventure and misadventure are legendary in the zombie hunter's community. This is mainly due to their professional work ethic and awesome clubhouse.

Many things separate the Jim Rage Elite Zombie Hunting Squad from the other organizations in this noble calling. The members' outrageous and colorful personalities top the list. The berserker attitude in the pitch of battle, the Pederby brothers' [some other high ranking members of the group] playful bickering, and our sense of humor when nothing seems funny … all of these make the organization different. Better? We think so. There is a sense of cooperation amongst all the zombie hunters and priorities are in order. That priority is to redead the undead, as Jim has said many times.

The details of Jim Rage's past are scant. It is known he is a master of weaponry and it is known he worked for a time with the CIA. During his stint with the government, Jim became acquainted with the man that was to become his mortal enemy. "Mr. Nighttime" was a member of a rogue faction of the EPA [Environmental Protection Agency]. He and his cadre, known only as the "Fifth Column," were engaged in experiments on the undead. The goal of the Fifth Column was to make a better soldier … using zombies. Anyone who has taken the oath to rid the world of the undead knows that this just isn't done.

Jim is a solitary man, shunning any and all public appearances. His whereabouts are generally unknown even to those closest to him. He is never out of touch with the organization or its members, however. Many attempts have been made on Jim's life. Most recently, in April 2006, at the annual company picnic a surprise attack from the Church of Death nearly wiped out the entire ranks of the Jim Rage Elite Zombie Hunting Squad. This was Jim's last public appearance. Only the key members survived. Their names include the Mad Hatter, Drew Peberdy, Ben Peberdy, and Baxter Black.

It was feared that everyone else was lost. In the charred rubble that was once a peaceful private gathering place, but was now a scene of smoking carnage, a survivor was found. That lucky man was me, "Wild West" Winfrey. My trademark leopard print Speedo was destroyed in the mayhem. I have another, but only wear it on special occasions.

The JREZHS, much like the Zombie Squad, also has a high level of dedication to community service. They sponsor a youth outreach program aimed at helping at-risk youths find constructive ways to escape their troubled lives. At JREZHS's regularly held outreach seminars, they reach out to teens by showing the value of self-expression through artistic creation. The leadership of JREZHS claim that they don't know how successful these seminars have been, but explain that the effort to improve the world is what ultimately matters.

When it comes to the actual purpose of the JREZHS organization, they have been kind enough to provide the following mission statement:

> We at Jim Rage's Elite Zombie Hunting Squadron believe above all else in the individual's ability to overcome all odds through simple focus and commitment. It is a fundamental truth that men and women can do absolutely anything if they put their minds to the task at hand and put in all their effort. There is nothing that is impossible. We also strongly support service to one's community. If everyone decided to help their neighbors with their problems, then not only would the world enjoy the benefits of unification and harmony, but everything would get done a lot quicker.

> Essentially, our mission at JREZHS is to connect with the youth of America and to encourage them to expand their minds and spirits and find pleasure in helping others and living a healthy lifestyle of moderation and balance—such as the ideals presented in Buddhist texts. We work closely with teenagers and support them in expressing themselves through art such as poetry, painting, drama, filmmaking, and photography. It is no big secret that teenagers are the future of America and the world. Thus, it is our moral and social obligation to ensure that they embrace philosophies of self-control, and come to know the rising and advancing of the spirit through art. They must be taught to understand the great worth of

supporting their communities. It is our belief that the negligence of teaching this value on the part of many parents has caused an untold hundreds of teenagers to be consumed by feelings of loneliness, alienation, anger, depression, and apathy.

There is no need for them to be forced to deal with such psychological pain and suffering, especially when they so often turn to dangerous drugs and the infliction of pain upon others as a release. We can work together to ensure that their lives are pleasant ones, in which they need not feel any guilt or fear in expressing their feelings and emotions to others. We can work together to ensure that they find happiness in helping others. We can help them to grow and become well-adjusted citizens. And by doing so, bring about a brighter and better future. Yes, we also kill zombies.

More information on the JREZHS, such as its membership and volunteer activities, can be accessed electronically at their website, www. jimrage.com.

The Zombie Survival and Defense Wiki

Most of us are by now familiar with the concept of a wiki, mainly due to the popularity of the convenient Internet resource Wikipedia. Well, the Zombie Survival and Defense Wiki (which can be found at zombiesurvivalwiki.com) is like a Wikipedia for zombie survivalists. Members of zombie survivalist organizations from all over the world have come together to contribute to this new, one-stop information resource on surviving a zombie apocalypse.

Need details on what melee/close-combat weapons have been tested and proven effective and durable? There's a page for that. Or perhaps you would like to see a list of the available zombie/disaster shelters in the world? Well, they have a page for that, too. Or maybe you need the specs on what kinds of power generators (diesel and unleaded) are right for your needs? If so, you are in luck. They have a page for that. Even if the zombie element was removed from the site, much of the information it provides would prove useful in just about any survival/disaster situation.

So You Wanna Be a Zombie Survivalist?

Perhaps you feel inspired to become a member of the zombie survivalist subculture yourself? Well, if so, you need to first decide what kind of group you are suited for. For example, some groups are mainly for fun, while others are serious about using zombies in order to promote the learning of real-world survival skills.

Brains!

If you are planning on starting your own zombie survivalist group, be sure you have the dedication needed to do so. For example, if your group will be selling items or making any revenue from its website, then you will need to register it as either a business entity or even a nonprofit organization. Not doing this has caused a number of such zombie groups to unexpectedly come under charges from the IRS.

If you are just looking for a novelty experience or a fun group to post to your MySpace or Facebook page, you would do best to find a suitable group on a social networking site. If you are serious about honing your survival skills while doing some good for the community, search the Internet for a group like the Zombie Squad. If a chapter is not available in your area, you might consider starting one.

Anyone Smell That?

Some zombie survivalist groups are more extreme than others. Some are just in it for a good time, while others are a bit more serious about it. Choose a group that best fits your personality. Also, it is always advisable to call a group you are considering joining *before* you just show up at one of their meetings both unprepared and uninformed.

Then again, maybe you have your own vision for what a zombie survivalist group should be. If so, you might start a zombie survivalist group of your own. This can be as easy as starting a group on Facebook. It can also be as complicated as creating your own organization and writing up specific rules, guidelines, and bylaws. The sky is the limit. However, you should know a few basic rules of conduct and etiquette, to avoid making any unintentional zombie survival faux-pas.

Rule #1: Every group is different, and it is considered bad form to criticize other zombie survivalist groups just because they don't run things in the same way your group does.

Rule #2: Follow the law! Keep it in perspective, because violating the law can quickly move your group from the Internet to the ATF and FBI watchlists.

Rule #3: Maintain your group/website. Every year, zombie survivalist groups are born only to die shortly thereafter due to the disinterest or negligence of the founder and/or members. If this is just a phase, you would do better to just join a group that is already being maintained.

Rule #4: It is all in good fun! Nobody likes a buzz-kill who always wants to argue about the little semantic details.

The Least You Need to Know

- Zombie survivalist groups are not (usually) a bunch of maniacs who think the world is doomed to the fate of a zombie apocalypse.
- The majority of zombie survivalists view zombies as a hypothetical scenario that helps them prepare for any real-life disaster possible.
- More than half of the zombie survivalist groups in the world can be found on social networking sites such as MySpace or Facebook.
- Many zombie survivalist groups are actively and frequently involved in community service projects.
- Some zombie survivalist groups focus more on fun and community service than on practical survival skills.
- If you are considering starting your own zombie survivalist group, remember to follow the four basic rules of conduct and etiquette.

Chapter 15

Bringing Down the Dead

In This Chapter

- The general consensus regarding zombie abilities and eating habits

- Why zombies are nothing like vampires

- Common beliefs regarding the anatomy of the walking dead

- A brief note on why zombies are so patient

- A look at some of the most effective (and ineffective) weapons when it comes to "redeading" the dead

- A training regimen for the hypothetical (we hope) zombie apocalypse

Some of the most interesting conversations in the world have begun with asking some variation of a seemingly innocent question: "Yeah, I know it's not real ... but what *if*?" Most of the information in this chapter is purely hypothetical (okay, just about all of it is hypothetical). Nonetheless, any treatment of zombies would be incomplete if the question of the zombie apocalypse (namely, how to survive it) is not at least addressed. Therefore, this chapter is meant to give you a basic foundation of the knowledge, equipment, and skills needed to survive the possibility of a zombie apocalypse.

Zombie Abilities and Eating Habits

When it comes to battling the undead, you need to get one thing into your head—zombies *do not* have *any* supernatural abilities. Well, that is, of course, unless you count being able to get up and move around after their hearts have stopped beating as a supernatural ability. But that's beside the point. According to the current general consensus, zombies are the result of a virus. They are not created by black magic or Voodoo, and they, in turn, have no unexplainable or paranormal abilities.

Mooooooaaaaan...

The abbreviation **RLF** stands for reanimated life form, which has become a term-savvy way of saying the "zed word" ... zombie. Honestly, however, this label doesn't exactly work. Think about it. A zombie isn't *alive*, so how in the world can it be called a *life* form? Anyway, you figure it out. If the world is ever overrun by undead flesh-eating hordes, there are obviously going to be far more important questions for you to consider than whether RLF is an appropriate classification for zombies.

A zombie, it is generally agreed, is incapable of possessing any abilities that it did not have during life. If anything, an *RLF* actually has fewer abilities than it did when it was a living human being. Since an RLF has lost the use of its neocortex, it has lost most of its cognitive thinking abilities, retaining only those that are connected to the instinct drives stored in the cerebral cortex, which is the control center of any human who has been reanimated.

Zombies and Brains

Do zombies eat brains? Well, the answer to this rather odd question can be both "yes" and "no." While a zombie is devouring some poor sap, if the eaten fellow's brains are within arm's reach and the RLF happens to snatch them up, it'll likely choose to eat the stuff. So, in that case, the answer to this question is "yes." However, this does not mean that zombies will actively *seek* to consume our gray matter. Zombies are not picky eaters, to say the least, and they have no greater preference for brains than they do for any other fleshy part of the human body.

As you read in Chapter 12, at some point back in the 1980s, a bunch of pop culture B-movie-makers created a slew of terrible zombie films in which the zombies could talk after their brains had been destroyed, although it would be impossible for a reanimated corpse to retain the ability of speech (because speaking requires thinking, which, in turn, requires you to have a somewhat fully functional brain). Pretty much the only sound these stinky flesh-addicts should be able to pull off would be a long, drawn-out moan or groan. Of course, they certainly *can* moan and groan at a variety of pitches and volumes (but that doesn't mean we should ask them to start a choir).

Brains!

> Zombies are generally believed to prefer the taste of human flesh (that is, of course, assuming that they can still taste *anything*). Some movies have presented the theory that this preference for live, warm human flesh may have something to do with a Zombie virus needing fresh DNA or some parasitic microorganism receiving some form of nourishment from live blood cells.

Second, the zombies in these frighteningly inaccurate films pursue and capture their victims before finally cracking their skulls open, at which point they begin scooping out their brains through a very neat and impossibly symmetrical circular hole in the head. What makes this even more ridiculous is that the zombies of these films are often able to accomplish this with nothing but their *bare hands*. Zombies are not even strong enough to break through a board of three-tiered plywood, but they have the strength to crack through the thick and dense bone of a human skull without so much as the tools or the slightest bit of difficulty?

Third, on a number of occasions in these films, people were bitten and thus infected with the zombie virus in places that were *nowhere* near the head. If zombies prefer to eat human brains, why in the world would they bite someone on the arm or leg (or anywhere other than the head, for that matter)? In fact, how would *anyone* become infected and reanimate to begin with if these zombies were motivated by a desire for human brains? If the only way to kill a zombie is to remove or destroy the brain (of course, in these films, even destroying the brain would not kill the zombies), and zombies started going around devouring the brains of everyone they ate, not a whole lot of people would ever reanimate after being eaten, would they? So perhaps the question presented in this section would be better stated as, "*Will* a zombie eat brains?" Yes, it will. However, "Do zombies prefer to eat *only* brains?" No, they don't.

Can Zombies Fly?

Unless an infected person dies and reanimates while he or she is aboard (or, worse, piloting) an airplane (in which case, you had better pray you are not on that flight), a zombie *cannot* fly.

As stated earlier, a zombie cannot display any ability it did not have when it was a living, breathing person. After going through the process of Z-virus reanimation, if anything, a zombie's range of abilities actually gets smaller with every passing moment. This ridiculous zombie untruth probably originates from the mythical Chinese creature known as the *Chiang-Shih* (see Chapter 3).

Zombies vs. Vampires

Zombies, simply put, *are not* vampires. They are not related to vampires (aside from the fact that both come back to life after death). They have nothing to do with vampires. In fact, it is likely that any self-respecting vampire would loathe the idea of even being compared to a creature as vile and gross as a zombie. Not that vampires aren't vile in their own ways, but zombies don't quite measure up to the level of danger posed by the sentient undead beings known as *homonus nocturnus*.

Vampires are a number of things (actually, they are everything) that zombies are *not*: amazingly fast, superhumanly strong, very difficult to kill, relatively intelligent at the least (though they more commonly exhibit above-average intelligence), and able to regenerate quickly.

Zombies, on the other hand, are ridiculously slow (a speed-walking grandma could easily outrun *most* zombies), rather weak (especially once rigor mortis starts to set in), easy to kill with almost any blunt object sturdy enough to crush through a skull, and about as dumb as carrots with legs. Furthermore, any wound or damage they receive is permanent.

Moooooaaaaan...

The label **homonus nocturnus** comes from Latin and is a classification for vampires recently coined by cryptozoology researchers. The term comes from the Latin words *homonus,* "humans" or "people," and *nocturnus,* which means "of night." So basically, the label translates as "humans of the night." However, since vampires aren't exactly "humans," per se, this label doesn't make a whole lot of sense, if you think about it very much.

This, of course, brings us to the enigmatic question: "In a fight between a zombie and a vampire, who would win?" And this is an excellent question, indeed. However, until someone actually manages to capture both a vampire and a zombie with which to run such a test, everyone will just have to keep on using their imaginations. However, if this hypothetical future fight ends up being a one-on-one match, you should probably put your money on the vampire.

Finally, if both vampires and zombies are created through the transmission of a virus, then what would happen to a vampire who became infected with the zombie virus? Perhaps even more puzzling is the question of how a zombie would be affected if it was infected with the virus that causes vampirism. What's more, would a zombie even be *affected* by this virus, since there are no living cells for such a micro-organism to attack (or even an active bloodstream to carry it)? Some theorize that the integration of these two viruses in a single *living* organism would create some kind of zombie-vampire hybrid. Others speculate that the result of such an experiment would more likely just be fatal to the person infected. However, even if such an experiment were in the realm of plausibility, who would be crazy enough to volunteer themselves as a test subject?

Zombies and Rigor Mortis

If a person were infected with a zombie virus and died from it, the amount of time it would take to reanimate is a matter of opinion at this point. Theories put the occurrence of reanimation at anywhere from a few minutes to several hours. Of course, no one can say anything for certain. However, what is agreed on is the fact that what reanimates will be nothing more than a *corpse*, a dead human body. Therefore, it can also be assumed that a zombie will be affected by most of the same elements that break down any run-of-the-mill, nonreanimated dead body: decomposition, insects/microorganisms (though some theorize that zombie flesh would be rejected by living organisms), weather, and (perhaps most importantly) *rigor mortis.*

Mooooooaaaaan...

> Rigor mortis (*rigor* means "stiffness" and *mortis* means "death") is a condition that affects a body after death, resulting in stiffening of muscles due in part to an extremely sharp drop in body temperature and the depletion of adenosine triphosphate (ATP), a substance in all living cells that provides energy for metabolic processes and is a crucial element in the production of ribonucleic acid (RNA) in muscle cells. Rigor mortis puts a corpse in a state of extreme rigidity roughly 24 hours following expiration of vital functions. However, it commonly goes away roughly 12 hours later.

Many diehard zombie fans point to the presence of rigor mortis for the argument against depictions of so-called "fast zombies." Basically, the idea is that the reanimated body of a zombie would have horrible damage inflicted to its muscles within the 12-hour-or-so rigor mortis period. This would happen because, despite the rigidity of the muscles during this period, a zombie's brain does not register pain and would therefore not detect any of the damage being caused by its forced movement. As a result, if a zombie experiencing rigor mortis were to set eyes on a living human target, it would still force itself to move. This forced movement would cause serious tissue damage, ripping muscle fibers and tearing tendons and ligaments with every step. By the time the rigor mortis had passed, a zombie's body would be so terribly damaged that many of its muscles would no longer work because many tendons would be torn completely loose from the bones. What muscles did still work would probably be pulling on weakened tendons, not to mention putting pressure on already damaged ligaments.

Since a reanimated zombie would not regenerate or heal, any damage done to its body would be totally permanent. This means that all zombies would, by some point, move slowly and awkwardly. Many point to this as the cause of the trademark "zombie limp," referred to as such because zombies are often depicted as dragging one limp leg behind them and their heads hanging to one side (the latter caused by damaged or snapped tendons and ligaments in the neck and shoulders), or they are shown with an arm that just dangles uselessly. A reanimated corpse that might appear to be moving awkwardly and slowly would actually be traveling at its *top speed* anytime it zeroes in on a living human target. As time goes on, any zombie's top speed would eventually be reduced to a crawl (and perhaps even to the point that it could no longer move).

The Recently Undead

Though most zombies would likely be weak, slow, and awkward in movement, this does not mean that all zombies would be this way. Despite the fact that the damage caused by rigor mortis would ruin any chances of zombies retaining the levels of strength and speed they had when alive, there is one thing that many have begun to consider—what would zombies be capable of *before* the rigidity of rigor mortis sets in?

During the hours before rigor mortis, it is generally believed that zombies would be at their most dangerous. They might, though rather briefly, even retain the strength and speed of a living human. These would be the most lethal adversaries during a zombie virus outbreak—those who had died and reanimated less than 18 hours ago, and especially those who had only just risen. This is why if one were to encounter a zombie at the moment of reanimation, it would be advisable to exterminate it without hesitation. Shoot it in the head. Bash its skull in with an ash tray, if you have to. But whatever you do, don't give it a chance to lock in on you as a target, or things will become a lot more difficult for you in a relatively short amount of time.

You may be wondering why, if rigor mortis begins roughly 24 hours after the body dies, would zombies be at their most dangerous for only the first *18* hours after reanimation? Well, as already explained, a zombie would not have the ability to heal—not even a little. Because of this, any physical activity that required even midlevel exertion—running, grabbing, jumping, climbing, pulling, or even standing up—would result in irreparable damage to the muscle tissue of the zombie.

You see, when a normal (living) human muscle performs physically demanding activities, the muscle cells are actually damaged by it. However, the healing process that follows creates more muscle cells, which, in turn, will cause the muscle as a whole to become stronger and bigger. The body of a zombie, on the other hand, would receive no such benefit. In fact, it would receive quite the opposite. Because of this, almost every movement a zombie made, whether or not rigor mortis had occurred, would cause permanent muscle tissue damage. By this rationale, it is likely that a zombie would have already done significant damage to its muscles within the initial 18 hours after its reanimation, thus slowing the thing down well before the more extreme, and ultimately crippling, damage of the rigor mortis period even began.

Zombies Are *Very* Patient

As mentioned previously in this book, one of the things that is frightening about zombies is the fact that they never seem to lose interest in eating people. This means that once one or more zombies have located you, even if they can't reach you, they aren't going anywhere unless distracted by a more accessible target. Unless this happens, their numbers would only grow with each passing hour as the sound of moaning from the zombies that have located you reach every other flesh-eater in earshot. This means that a few will soon turn into a few dozen, and a few dozen would become a few hundred before you know it.

This is what makes zombies dangerous. The number of zombies will only continue to increase at an exponential rate until we living human beings begin working together, collectively, to exterminate them. Unfortunately, the odds are rather poor that this would occur in time to prevent a global infestation of reanimated corpses. In which case, it looks like you will probably be on your own when and if the living dead come knocking at your door. So you might want to arm yourself.

Zombie Weapons

Putting down a zombie isn't complicated. If you destroy the brain, you destroy the zombie. Of course, the weapons with which this can be done are various. For the most part, two primary forms of weaponry are used in the "redeading" of the undead—firearms and melee/close-combat weapons. The number one rule to follow when it comes to weaponry is simple: *follow the law*. When choosing your weapons, consider four elements:

◆ **Legality:** Can you carry the weapon in the open without risking arrest?

◆ **Functionality:** Is the weapon durable enough to withstand prolonged combat? Are you able to wield it with a fair amount of ability?

◆ **Portability:** Will the weight of the weapon make it a burden to carry over long distances?

◆ **Noise level:** Is the weapon unnecessarily loud, and will it attract the attention of other zombies in the area?

When it comes to melee/close-combat weapons, here are some suggestions that meet all these criteria:

◆ **Crowbar or tire iron:** Both are perfectly legal, very durable, easy to wield (though you might wrap them with athletic tape, if possible, to avoid slippage), and small enough to carry on your hip.

◆ **Hammer:** Again, this is legal and convenient. The one-handed type is suggested (avoid sledgehammers, as they are too heavy and unwieldy).

◆ **Hatchet:** Fairly legal in the right circumstances, and very convenient for travel. Again, the one-handed type is best (not a full-sized axe, which is problematic for the same reasons as sledgehammers).

◆ **Baseball bat:** Legal, though less simple to carry, unless you fashion some sort of carrier. Wood bats are recommended (the soft metal aluminum bats tend to bend easily).

◆ **Axe handles:** Semilegal, depending on the circumstances (there's no specific law against carrying axe handles), these are highly durable. However, they have the same carry issues as baseball bats.

Don't Get Bit!

> The durability of any wooden weapon can be greatly multiplied by sanding it down and immersing it in Tung Oil for four to six hours, then wiping it clean. Upholstery studs work well for reinforcing striking points. Athletic tape and skateboard grip tape are also good materials for reinforcing wooden weapons or for equipping handles so they don't slip on sweaty palms.

As far as firearms are concerned, the more generic, the better. Specialized guns usually mean specialized ammunition. In a world where you'll need to take ammo as you come across it, you want a weapon with generic ammunition. For example, a .50-caliber Desert Eagle handgun may have a lot of stopping power. However, the ammo is expensive and rarer than most. Not to mention that such a powerful round makes one heck of a bang. The best calibers and weapon types are as follows:

◆ **.22-caliber rifle:** This is the preferred weapon of assassins for a reason. It's lightweight and accurate from a distance, and it makes a minimal noise even without a silencer. The ammo is fairly small, which means you can carry more of it.

◆ **9mm pistol:** The 9mm ammo is probably one of the most generic rounds in the modern world. Most police officers carry some form of 9mm as a service weapon.

◆ **.38-caliber revolver:** This caliber is almost always seen in revolvers, which means you have six to seven shots before you have to reload. Next to 9mm, this is the most common round for police service revolvers.

◆ **10- or 12-gauge shotgun:** Twelve-gauge rounds are more common than 10. Shotguns are excellent zombie-fighting weapons at mid- to close range and require less marksmanship skill because they shoot a wide spread of projectiles. However, they are useless at a distance and make a lot of noise.

Training for Zombies

Your level of physical fitness has a major impact on your chances of survival, not just in a zombie apocalypse, but in any disaster situation. Zombies, however, would require an especially high level of endurance, coupled with a very specific set of physical skills. Considering this, what follows is a training regimen specifically designed to prepare an individual for a zombie apocalypse. Since most of us will probably need to start slow and work our way up, the workouts are divided into two four-week sections, with increasing levels of intensity.

Beginner Zombie Fitness

Depending on your personal fitness level, you may or may not need to begin this schedule at Week 1. However, it is better to start slowly than it is to push yourself so hard that you injure yourself. An injury will only slow you down further, so be sensible and, if need be, start at the beginning. And some of us may need to stay at the Week 1 pace for longer than just a week, which is fine.

Each workout is to be done per day, with rest days between as needed.

Week 1: 4–6 days, 1–3 rest days

♦ 30-minute walk (at a brisk but comfortable pace)

♦ 5 sets of pushups (no more than 30-second rests in between, if at all), in the following order

1×5 repetitions

1×4 reps

1×3 reps

2×2 reps

♦ 25 jumping jacks

Week 2: 5–6 days, 1–2 rest days

♦ 2- to 5-minute jog, followed by 25-minute walk

♦ 5 sets of pushups

1×10

1×8

1×6

2×4

◆ 30 jumping jacks

Week 3: 6 days, 1 rest day

◆ 5- to 7-minute jog, followed by 25-minute walk

◆ 5 sets of pushups

1×15

1×10

1×8

2×6

◆ 40 jumping jacks

Week 4: 6 days, 1 rest day

◆ 7- to 10-minute jog, followed by 20- to 25-minute walk

◆ 5 sets of pushups

1×20

1×15

1×10

2×7

◆ 50 jumping jacks

Advanced Zombie Fitness Regimen

Don't undertake this part of the routine until you can complete the Week 4 regimen in the beginner fitness section with a relative amount of proficiency. Basically, if the Week 4 workout is still kicking your butt, you should probably stay at that level until it isn't. Remember, the goal is to make yourself stronger … not to get yourself injured.

Week 5: 6 days, 1 rest day

- 15-minute jog, followed by 15- to 20-minute walk
- 2 sets (*not* 5) of pushups

  1×50

  1×15
- 50 jumping jacks
- 5 pull-ups, or 15 elbow drags (to do an elbow drag, lay on your stomach, clasp your hands together, reach out, and use your elbows to drag your body forward)

Week 6: 6 days, 1 rest day

- 20-minute jog, followed by 15- to 20-minute walk
- 2 sets (*not* 5) of pushups

  1×50

  1×20
- 50 jumping jacks
- 10 pull-ups or 25 elbow drags

Week 7: 6 days, 1 rest day

- 25-minute jog, followed by 25-minute walk
- 2 sets (*not* 5) of pushups

  1×50

  1×25
- 50 jumping jacks
- 15 pull-ups or 30 elbow drags

Week 8: 6 days, 1 rest day

◆ 2- to 5-minute sprint, followed by a 25-minute jog, followed by a 15- to 20-minute walk

◆ 2 sets (*not* 5) of pushups

1×50

1×40

◆ 20–25 pull-ups or 50 elbow drags

Once you have reached the point where you can complete the Week 8 routine with a fair amount of proficiency, you should also try to begin taking lessons or at least practicing with your melee weapon of choice. Remember, swinging a baseball bat, crowbar, or tire iron can become pretty tiring, and exhaustion can lead to clumsiness in your technique. The best way to avoid this is to practice with your close-combat weapon of choice until it becomes an extension of your body.

Beware!

> The statutes regarding items that can potentially be used as weapons change from state to state. For example, in some states it is illegal to carry a baseball bat in your vehicle unless it is accompanied by a ball and glove. There are also jurisdictions where an officer can arrest a person for carrying a crowbar without a valid reason, as it is a tool often used by burglars to gain entry into homes.

However, you should also remember to follow the law. Be sure that the close-combat weapon you have chosen is legal in your state of residence. Nothing puts a damper on weapons training like getting yourself arrested for practicing with an illegal weapon in full view of your neighbors. On another note, melee weapons training is probably an activity best done in the privacy of your home, garage, or backyard (or, if applicable, your martial arts gym or karate dojo).

Whatever You Do ... Do It Fast!

There are multiple schools of thought as to what immediate actions would be the best during the initial outbreak of a zombie apocalypse.

Some believe that finding a safe place in which to hide until the chaos and panic of the initial moments of the apocalypse subside is the best way to go. Others believe that the best way to survive the ever-growing hordes of the undead is to stay in constant motion. However, everyone agrees on at least one thing—whatever you do, you should do it fast. It is generally understood by enthusiasts of the zombie apocalypse scenario that the sooner a person begins taking steps to survive, the better his or her chances of succeeding.

Before we start discussing the possible steps one could or should take, let us first discuss what *not* to do. In the event of a zombie outbreak, it is hypothesized that certain locations (many of which would otherwise be seen as safe) will be "hotspots" for zombie infection. Such dangerous locales include, but are not limited to:

◆ **Hospitals:** After all, the first wave of people who are attacked or bitten by zombies will head straight for the nearest emergency rooms. In fact, just about any emergency medical facility would likely turn into a tasty flesh buffet within the first 24 hours of the zombie apocalypse.

◆ **Police stations:** One would normally think of a police station as the safest place to go in the event of danger. In a zombie apocalypse, however, it will become a deathtrap. Many of the first people bitten or attacked will mistakenly think they've been victims of assaults, and about half of them will go to the police station to file reports. People also feel safer knowing police are near, and so will head to stations for protection. Lastly, if you're unlucky enough to have to bash in the head of a zombie before the general public knows what is happening, the cops might consider you a criminal and lock you up. And, as one might expect, being locked up in a jail cell is not a good place to be during a zombie apocalypse.

◆ **Churches:** There is something about a zombie apocalypse that brings out the spiritual side in people. Some will even view it as a sign of some religious Armageddon. Confused and afraid, many will flock to spiritual centers in order to be comforted, to pray, and to make their final confessions when they see death coming over the horizon.

◆ **Malls or department stores:** While these places will become valuable sources for looting once the initial chaos subsides, at first they will be dangerous madhouses. When the fecal matter hits the fan, people tend to get kind of nuts about the essentials—like food, water, and gasoline. Not to mention that the general state of incivility is bound to bring looters and various criminals out of the woodwork. While zombie infection is present in these places, it is people in general that will make them dangerous.

So what plan of action would be the most advisable? Well, since none of these zombie plans have ever been field tested, no one can really say for certain. For the most part, the initial stage of any zombie plan you may hear of is most likely going to be some sort of variation on any one of the following three potential options:

◆ "Moving Target" strategy

◆ Fortification

◆ Fall back and fortify plan

The "Moving Target" Strategy

The "Moving Target" strategy, as we shall refer to it, is what its name suggests—you start moving and do your best to stop only if necessary. This strategy is based on the idea that, while zombies will surround a static location in growing numbers, they are too slow and physically weak to keep up with a constantly moving target. Therefore, supporters of this strategy claim that, upon becoming aware of a zombie outbreak, one should immediately acquire a vehicle, stock up on as much fuel as possible, and hit the road.

While it is true that zombies would have little to no chance of keeping up with almost any modern vehicle, there is a flaw to this plan. In times of disaster, whether it be a riot, high-power earthquake, flooding, or an approaching hurricane, everybody in the area usually has the same idea at about the same time—to get the heck out of town. Before you know it, gas stations will be saturated with commuters trying to stock up on gas. The roadways out of the area will be choked with traffic, turning these potential means of escape into worthless tin cans. And if a horde of zombies finds its way onto a congested roadway where traffic is at a standstill, you can rest assured that *everybody* is going to get out of their vehicles and run for their lives. These abandoned vehicles will soon render the modern roads and freeways of nearly every major city useless.

Granted, if one resides in a small town or rural area, where people tend to be more spread out than they are in the cities, then the "Moving Target" strategy becomes a bit more plausible. In a rural environment, one could theoretically avoid being surrounded by the living dead by simply changing one's location by as little as a few miles every hour or two. If one was the owner of some form of mobile living accommodations, such as a camper trailer or motor coach (more commonly referred to as a "tour bus"), then one could maintain this strategy for as long as one's available fuel supply holds out—which brings us to the next issue with the "Moving Target" strategy.

With any of these three potential options, you really have to decide if you are going to just have a strategy ... or if you are going to have a plan. What is the difference, you ask? Well those who just use this method as a strategy will eventually find themselves stranded without fuel. Those who adopt this strategy and *plan* for it will have already stocked up with enough fuel to allow them time to find more after the initial wave of desperate mobs has subsided (or been eaten).

Anyone Smell That?

The devil is in the details, it is often said. And something like automatic locks can pose an unexpected danger in emergency situations. For example, many of today's vehicles will automatically open all the doors on a car when the driver's side door is unlocked with a key. This means that the owner has no way of entering the car without running the risk of having one of the other three doors opened. This is why manual door locks would be preferable, since you cannot accidentally unlock them.

Someone who just decides to use this strategy is likely to simply use whatever car he or she currently owns, no matter how totally unsuited it may be for the requirements of the situation at hand. Someone who has already planned to use this strategy will have acquired a properly designed vehicle. It won't need to be too big, as this will make it hard to get through narrow obstacles. And although four-wheel drive is optional, it is highly recommended since, as already mentioned, most roads will be rendered impassable. The car will also need to be modified for the situation. For example, the windows will need some way to be reinforced. The locks should be manual, not electronic, since this is less likely to cause awkwardly dangerous situations.

Fortification

Many zombie survival enthusiasts consider the basic "fortification" strategy as nothing more than the hasty, instinctual reaction of an unprepared individual. With no plan of action, it is human nature to get home, lock the doors, bar the windows, and defend one's property and loved ones. Any aboveground structure, however, no matter how well fortified and supplied it may be, will only be good for as long as the undead don't know you are in there.

Remember the Alamo? Hastily fortifying your home can often turn into a zombified reenactment of the same scenario. For the sake of argument, think of a guy who rushes home to arm himself with whatever firearm he may own. He secures his family inside and barricades the doors and windows, making a terrible amount of noise in the process and attracting the attention of every walking corpse within earshot. As he peers through the space between the boards that now cover his windows, he sees that a number of zombies are heading for his house. Unable to shoot through the barricades, he makes his way to an upstairs window. He may even manage to get onto the roof. He loads up his weapon and begins picking off the approaching zombies. What he is really doing, however, is sending out dinner bells to every zombie for blocks. With every air-shattering blast of gunfire, the man would in actuality only be adding another nail to his own coffin. For every zombie he kills, he has probably attracted two or three more to his location.

Soon enough, the power grid goes down. He doesn't have a generator and does not own an emergency radio (as far fewer people do these days than in the past). He is cut off from the outside world. No phone. No computer/Internet. No radio. Soon what food there was in the fridge has begun to spoil and he is unable to venture out to look for supplies because his home is surrounded by dozens of zombies. Eventually, things are going to fall apart. Perhaps at some point he uses up his supply of recreational ammunition and so he is unable to hold back the mass of human bodies crashing against his doors. Or perhaps the boards on the windows finally begin to give way under the strain of so many clawing hands. No matter how it happens, have no doubt that at some point they are going to get in. Once this happens, our hypothetical subject's ill-fated last stand will end for him in the same way the last stand at the Alamo ended for the men who defended it—everyone inside is going to die.

Now, this does not mean that the use of a fortification is completely useless. If timed correctly in its use, and as long as it is not treated as a permanent solution, the use of a fortified structure could save your life—especially during the first few days of the outbreak. Some say that it is best to go to a sturdy structure and remain hidden for anywhere from 3 to 14 days, or however long it takes for things to calm down a bit. Once this occurs (and only then), you emerge from your place of hiding and attempt to venture out from the area ... which brings us to the third and final potential plan.

Fall Back and Fortify Plan

You may notice that this option is referred to as a *plan*, not a strategy. This is because there is no way to carry this method out without planning ahead (at least, not with any good chance of success). This plan consists of two primary phases, the first of which may need to be undertaken after an initial period of hiding depending on your particular situation:

- **Fall back:** Retreat from the area as quickly as possible, preferably before the general public starts going nuts, and proceed directly to a predetermined location

- **Fortify:** Establish no less than three fortified locations

The first phase of the plan is self-explanatory. The second, however, is a bit more complicated and requires planning. The idea is that you should buy a plot of rural land (the more rural the better) big enough to hold three to five structures far enough apart to be out of sight from one another. Another option is to purchase (or at least locate) several cabins in well-separated locations. The reason you need multiple locations is two-fold.

First of all, if you arrive at one location and find it unusable due to such things as the presence of zombies or even violent humans, you can simply head for one of the others. It is thought that zombies would try to explore anything that resembles a human residence in search of food (that's you), but that they will leave once they discover no one is inside. Therefore, by temporarily using another location, you would open up the possibility that the first structure will again be usable in the future.

Anyone Smell That?

Would zombies have any form of memory? Well, the jury is still out on that, obviously, since the dead have not yet risen to feed on the flesh of the living. Some speculate, however, that they would. This would be both a positive and negative for the living. Since they retain memory, zombies would eventually stop searching places for food after doing so unsuccessfully so many times. This means that, in time, one could occupy a single location for a longer period of time. The downside is that memory is also the basic attribute of *learning*, which means that zombies could in time discover the use of such things as tools or weapons. They might even learn the benefit of pack hunting, or begin to use rudimentary strategies such as ambushes.

The second reason for having multiple locations is because, as already explained, one of the undead is almost guaranteed to discover you. When this happens, it will let out a moan that will bring any other zombie in the area straight to you. Instead of "pulling an Alamo" by using a firearm to pick off the first few zombies, with this plan you have a much better option. Using melee weapons, you can dispatch the small initial group of zombies, and thereby avoid alerting any additional undead to your whereabouts. You would then have at least a brief period of time to load any essential supplies into your vehicle and head for one of the other locations.

This plan solves the problem of the "Moving Target" strategy, since it cuts down on the consumption of fuel that would occur if you were to live solely in your car. It also cuts down on the potential for "pulling an Alamo" as is likely to happen with the basic fortification strategy. This plan, if well mapped out and properly prepared for, would offer you the best of both worlds. You would have the ability to reside in a defensible location (vehicles, by the way, make terrible defense structures ... especially if they are out of gas) and still have the ability to remain mobile while using a minimal amount of your now oh-so-precious gasoline.

The Least You Need to Know

◆ Zombies have no supernatural abilities and are fairly weak and awkward.

◆ It is theorized that recently reanimated zombies would briefly retain close to the same level of strength and speed they had when alive.

◆ No matter what weapon you decide to use, always consider legality, functionality, portability, and noise level.

◆ Never rely on any close-combat weapon unless you have personally and rigorously tested its durability and are certain it can withstand prolonged combat.

◆ Generic weapons are always preferable to custom or rare firearms with rarer forms of ammunition.

◆ Your physical fitness level will have a big impact on your odds of surviving anything, zombies or otherwise.

Appendix A

Further Reading

In this appendix you will find a list of available book titles that should prove useful in furthering your education in the world of the living dead, no matter what form you might choose for it to take. From cinema history, to spirituality, to survival—even to sociology and philosophy—you can find zombies everywhere. What follows is a sampling of the available zombie-related titles.

Bourne, J. L. *Day by Day Armageddon*. Jefferson City: Permuted Press, 2009.

Brooks, Max. *World War Z: An Oral History of the Zombie War*. New York: Three Rivers Press, 2007.

———. *The Zombie Survival Guide*. New York: Three Rivers Press, 2003.

———. *The Zombie Survival Guide: Recorded Attacks*. New York: Three Rivers Press, 2009.

Brown, Nathan Robert, and Robert Anthony Fox. *Dead Come Home*. Scotts Valley: Create Space, 2009.

Cordray, Robert. *Zombies 101: Knowledge Is Survival*. Frederick: Publish America, 2008.

Curran, Bob. *Encyclopedia of the Undead*. Franklin Lakes: Career Press, 2009.

————. *Zombies: A Field Guide to the Walking Dead*. Franklin Lakes: New Page Books, 2008.

Dendle, Peter. *The Zombie Movie Encyclopedia*. Jefferson: McFarland and Company, 2000.

Flint, David. *Zombie Holocaust: How the Living Dead Devoured Pop Culture*. Medford: Plexus Publishing, 2009.

Grahame-Smith, Seth. *Pride and Prejudice and Zombies: The Classic Regency Romance—Now with Ultra-Violent Zombies!* Philadelphia: Quirk Books, 2009.

Greene, Richard, and Silem Mohammad. *The Undead and Philosophy: Chicken Soup for the Soulless*. Chicago: Open Court, 2006.

Jolly, Martyn. *Faces of the Living Dead*. New York: Mark Batty Publisher, 2006.

Kay, Glenn, and Stuart Gordon. *Zombie Movies: The Ultimate Guide*. Chicago: Chicago Review Press, 2008.

Kenemore, Scott. *The Zen of Zombie: Better Living Through the Undead*. New York: Skyhorse Publishing, 2007.

Ma, Roger. *The Zombie Combat Manual*. New York: Berkeley Trade, 2010.

Maberry, Jonathan. *Zombie CSU: Forensics of the Living Dead*. New York: Citadel Press, 2008.

Marco, Meghann. *Field Guide to the Apocalypse: Movie Survival Skills for the End of the World*. New York: Simon Spotlight Entertainment, 2005.

McIntosh, Shawn. *Zombie Culture: Autopsies of the Living Dead.* Lanham: Scarecrow Press, 2008.

Mecum, Ryan. *Zombie Haiku: Good Poetry for Your … Brains.* Cincinnati: How Publishing, 2008.

Paffenroth, Kim. *Dying to Live: A Novel of Life Among the Undead.* Jefferson City: Permuted Press, 2007.

———. *Gospel of the Living Dead: George Romero's Visions of Hell on Earth.* Waco, TX: Baylor University Press, 2006.

———. *History Is Dead: A Zombie Anthology.* Jefferson City: Permuted Press, 2007.

Rhodes, Gary Don. *White Zombie: Anatomy of a Horror Film.* Jefferson: McFarland and Company, 2001.

Russell, Jamie. *Book of the Dead: The Complete History of Zombie Cinema.* England, UK: FAB Press, 2005.

Russo, John. *Night of the Living Dead.* Alberta, Canada: Commonwealth Publications Inc., 1997.

Wadsworth, Jennifer. *Diary of a Grammar Zombie.* Indianapolis: Wiley Publishing, 2008.

Appendix B

Zombie Organizations and Resources

If this book has whetted your appetite for all things zombie, don't stop here. The Internet is overflowing with sites dedicated to the subject of the walking dead. From zombie film databases to literature, from survivalist groups to discussion forums, there is no shortage of zombies on the web.

There are two main lists in this appendix. The first is a list of the many zombie survivalist groups currently in operation. The second list offers sites related to zombie fandom as well as other resources for information on the living dead, such as games, movies, and the usual hypothetical discussions.

Zombie Survivalist Groups

Anti-Zombie Attack Squad   http://azasquad.com

Anti-Zombie League   www.antizombieleague.org

Federal Vampire and Zombie Agency (The Vanguard)   http://FVZA.org

Jim Rage's Elite Zombie Hunting Squad   http://jimrage.com

National Center for Reanimation Prevention and Control (NCRPC) http://michael.tresca.net/ncrpchome.html

Order of Zombie Outbreak Resistance Tacticians (OZORT) http://OZORT.org

The Swiss Cheese and Bullets Rescue and Response Team (SCB) http://zombie-egg.com

Zombie Defense Coalition www.thezdc.org

Zombie Defense Force http://zombiedefenseforce.com

Zombie Defense Organization http://zombiedefense.org

Zombie Defense Training http://zombiedefense.blogspot.com

Zombie Emergency Defense (ZED) http://zombiesafezone.com

Zombie Emergency Response Organization (ZERO) www.zombieemergencyresponseorganization.com

Zombie Escape Plan Headquarters www.zombieescapeplan.com

Zombie Preparedness Initiative ww2.Zombieinitiative.org

Zombie Meter www.zombiemeter.org

Zombie Militia Online Forum http://zombiemilitia.com

Zombie Squad, Inc. (multiple chapters in the United States) http://zombiehunters.org

Zombies Are Coming www.zombiesarecoming.com

Zombie Resources and Fandom Groups

Buy Zombie (a site for zombie merchandise) www.buyzombie.com

Dead On **Official Site** (bio-documentary of George A. Romero) http://georgeromerodoc.com

Homepage of the Dead (George A. Romero fan site) www.homepageofthedead.com

Intramural Zombie Hunting League http://SEIBEI.com/shop/intramural.html

Official Machete Zombie Fan Site www.machetezombie.com

Shoot for the Head www.shootforthehead.com

Tales of the Zombie War (Max Brooks fan site) http://talesofworldwarz.com

W. Doug Bolden, On Zombies www.wyrmis.com/zombies.html

The Zombie Hub and Zombie Network www.zombiehub.com

Zombie Info (horror/zombie cinema site) www.zombieinfo.com

Zombie Portraits (by artist Rob Sacchetto) www.zombieportraits.com

Zombie Threat Level: Assessing the Apocalypse www.zombiethreatlevel.com

Zombies Outside (fantasy site) http://zombiesoutside.com

Other Zombie Web Resources

All Things Zombie http://allthingszombie.com

House of Zombie: Your Guide to Living the Undead Lifestyle www.houseofzombie.com

Humans vs. Zombies (the official game site) http://humansvszombies.org

I Love the Undead: We Are the Zombie Nation http://ilovetheundead.blogspot.com

Kill the Zombies (a site offering free online zombie games) www.killthezombies.com

The Official King Zombie Site http://kingzombie.com

The Super Zombie Store http://superzombiestore.com

Top Zombie Sites web-list http://zombie.top-site-list.com

The Undead Report http://undeadreport.com

Web Zombies www.webzombies.com

Zombie Alert Home Protection Systems (offers a $1,000,000 guarantee) www.loris.net/zombie

Zombie Ammo (offering the latest in zombie shooting targets and apparel) www.zombieammo.com

The Zombie Channel   www.zombiechannel.com

The Zombie Club (zombie film fan site)   http://zombieclub.com

Zombie Costumes   http://zombiecostume.net

Zombie CSU Official Website   http://zombiecsu.com

The Zombie Dump   http://zombiedump.com

Zombie Friends: A Place for Horror (a zombie-themed social networking site)   www.zombiefriends.com

Zombie Lore: Zombies, as Nature Intended   http://zombielore.com

The Zombie Lovers   www.zombielovers.com

Zombie Mall: For When All Hell Breaks Loose!   http://zombiemall.com

Zombie Makeover   www.zombiemakeover.com

Zombie Maker: The Definitive Zombie Makeup and Costume Guide   www.zombiemaker.com

Zombie Movie Reviews Home Page   www.zombiemoviereviews.com

Zombie Movies Home Page   http://zombiemovies.org

Zombie Pin-Ups: Beauty and Braaains!   www.zombiepinups.com

Zombie Popcorn (zombie films site)   http://zombie-popcorn.com

Zombie Portraits: The Gift That Keeps on Living   www.zombieportraits.com

Zombie Rama   www.zombierama.com

The Zombie Reporting Center   www.zombiereportingcenter.com

Zombie Survival and Defense Wiki   www.zombiesurvivalwiki.com

Zombie Walk: Your Source for Zombie Walk and Zombie Flash Mob Planning   www.zombiewalk.com

The Zombie Watch Network   www.zombiewatchnetwork.com

Zombie World News   http://zombieworldnews.com

The ZombiePhiles   www.zombiephiles.com

Zombies Bite   www.zombiesbite.com

Index

D

Night of the Flesh Eaters, 124
Night of the Living Dead, 22,
   124–132
   characters, 130
   copyrights, 124
   Escape of the Living Dead and, 86
   human interaction, 129
   mistakes humans made, 41
   public domain, 125
   remake, 169
   "They're coming to get you
      Barbara," 127
   zombies' fear of fire, 129
Night of the Living Dead 3D, 169
"Night" zombies, 26
Nihonto (Japanese sword), 85
Norse *Draugar*, 35–36

O

offensive actions against zombies,
   48
Ojibwa/Chippewa *Baykok*, 36–37
Oliver-Martin, Tom, 99
organized zombies, 84
origins of fictional monsters, 20
origins of zombies, 19
Ouanga, 111–113
outlaw of practice of Zombie-ism, 5

P–Q

p-zombies, 48
Paffenroth, Kim, 74
Partial Test Ban Treaty, 21
patience of zombies, 202
Pegg, Simon, 154
people buried alive, revenants, 34
Phillips, Sean, 82
philosophical zombies, 48–50
places to avoid, 209–210
police stations, 209

preparedness, 184
   fall back and fortify plan,
      213–214
   fortification strategy, 212
   supplies, 184
Pride and Prejudice and Zombies,
   68, 75
primal myth, 7
Prometheus, 55
puffer fish dangers, 7
puffer fish neurotoxin, 6
punishment for going against
   community, 9

R

radiation, 23
   fear, 21
   fiction world's reaction, 22
   Night of the Living Dead, 22
   as nuclear boogeyman, 22
rage virus (*28 Days Later*), 151
reanimation
   Frankenstein's monster, 56
   Herbert West: Reanimator, 58
   time until, 200–202
recent literature
   Book of the Dead, 68
   City of the Dead, 68, 71
   Dead Come Home, 75
   Dead World, 75
   *Death Troopers: Recovered
      Messages from Purge*, 77
   *Dying to Live: A Novel of Life
      Among the Undead*, 74
   Pride and Prejudice and Zombies,
      68, 75
   The Rising, 68–70
   Star Wars: Death Troopers, 76
   Still Dead: Book of the Dead 2, 68
   World War Z, 71–73
   Zombie Haiku, 68, 77–78

S